By Ariel Levy

THE RULES DO NOT APPLY

FEMALE CHAUVINIST PIGS

The

Rules

Do Not

Apply

The Rules Do Not Apply

Ariel Levy

A

MEMOIR

RANDOM HOUSE

NEW YORK

Published in the United States by Random House, an imprint and division of Penguin Random House LLC, New York.

RANDOM HOUSE and the HOUSE colophon are registered trademarks of Penguin Random House LLC.

This work is based on "Thanksgiving in Mongolia" by Ariel Levy, which originally appeared in *The New Yorker*, November 18, 2013.

Grateful acknowledgment is made to Sony/ATV Music Publishing for permission to reprint an excerpt from "Beginning of a Great Adventure" by Michael Rathke and Lou Reed, copyright © 1988 Metal Machine Music and EMI Screen Gems. All rights administered by Sony/ATV Music Publishing, 424 Church Street, Suite 1200, Nashville, TN 37219. All rights reserved. Reprinted by permission.

LIBRARY OF CONGRESS CATALOGING-IN-PUBLICATION DATA
NAMES: Levy, Ariel, author.
TITLE: The rules do not apply / Ariel Levy.
DESCRIPTION: First edition. | New York : Random House, 2017.
IDENTIFIERS: LCCN 2016043502| ISBN 9780812996937 (hardback : acid-free paper) | ISBN 9780812996944 (ebook)
SUBJECTS: LCSH: Levy, Ariel. | Levy, Ariel—Marriage. | Women journalists—United States—Biography. | Young women—United States—Biography. | Miscarriage—United States. | Lesbians—United States—Biography. | Sex role—United States. | Life change events—United States. | BISAC: BIOGRAPHY & AUTOBIOGRAPHY / Personal Memoirs. | SOCIAL SCIENCE / Lesbian Studies.
CLASSIFICATION: LCC CT275.L3777 A3 2017 | DDC 305.30973—dc23
LC record available at https://lccn.loc.gov/2016043502

Printed in the United States of America on acid-free paper

randomhousebooks.com

987654321

FIRST EDITION

Book design by Barbara M. Bachman

For

AEN & EJJS

DO YOU EVER TALK TO YOURSELF? I DO IT ALL THE TIME. *We* do it, I should say, because that's how it sounds in my head. When I'm following a map, for instance: *We're going to turn right on Vicolo del Leopardo, go past the bar with the mosaic tiles, and then we know where we are.* It's an old habit: *We're going to look the teacher in the eye and tell her it's not fair.* My competent self is doing the talking; my bewildered self is being addressed. *We're going to go over to the phone now and call for help with one hand and hold the baby with the other.*

For the first time I can remember, I cannot locate my competent self—one more missing person. In the last few months, I have lost my son, my spouse, and my house. Every morning I wake up and for a few seconds I'm disoriented, confused as to why I feel grief seeping into my body, and then I remember what has become of my life. I am thunderstruck by feeling at odd times, and then I find myself gripping the kitchen counter, a subway pole, a friend's body, so I won't fall over. I don't mean that figuratively. My sorrow is so intense it often feels like it will flatten me.

It's all so over-the-top. Am I in an Italian opera? A Greek tragedy? Or is this just a weirdly grim sitcom? A few weeks ago, my neighbors came by my house on Shelter Island; they wanted to meet the baby. He's dead, I had to tell them. I felt bad, because what are they supposed to say to that? They said, We're so sorry. They said, Soon it will be summer and you can work in your beautiful garden. Not exactly, I explained. We have to sell the house; I'm here to pack up. (I know: those poor people.) They were silent as they searched for something safe to land on, and then they asked where my spouse was. I didn't have the heart to tell them.

As it happened, on that day I was even angrier than usual with the person I'd lived with for a decade, who'd said that the key to our Jeep would be waiting for me taped underneath the engine by the driver's-side tire. The car was in Greenport, New York, across the Peconic Bay from our house, in the parking lot where we always left it when we went away because that's where the bus drops you off. I got a ride out there from the city with some friends in the pouring rain, but none of us could find that key. I lay on my back with the rain coming down hard on my legs, the scent of wet asphalt rising around me, and I stared up at the underbelly of the Jeep, searching for something that wasn't there.

Until recently, I lived in a world where lost things could always be replaced. But it has been made overwhelmingly clear to me now that anything you think is yours by right can vanish, and what you can do about that is nothing at all. The future I thought I was meticulously crafting for years has disappeared, and with it have gone my ideas about the kind of life I'd imagined I was due.

People have been telling me since I was a little girl that I was too fervent, too forceful, *too much*. I thought I had harnessed the power of my own strength and greed and love in a life that could contain it. But it has exploded.

Part
One

1

MY FAVORITE GAME WHEN I WAS A CHILD WAS MUMMY
and Explorer. My father and I would trade off roles: One of
us had to lie very still with eyes closed and arms crossed
over the chest, and the other had to complain, "I've been
searching these pyramids for so many years—when will I
ever find the tomb of Tutankhamun?" (This was in the late
seventies when Tut was at the Met, and we came in from
the suburbs to visit him frequently.) At the climax of the
game, the explorer stumbles on the embalmed Pharaoh
and—brace yourself—the mummy opens his eyes and
comes to life. The explorer has to express shock, and then
say, "So, what's new?" To which the mummy replies, "*You.*"

I was not big on playing house. I preferred make-believe
that revolved around adventure, starring pirates and knights.
I was also domineering, impatient, relentlessly verbal, and,
as an only child, often baffled by the mores of other kids. I
was not a popular little girl. I played Robinson Crusoe in a
small wooden fort my parents built from a kit in the back-

yard, where I sorted through the acorns and onion grass I gathered for sustenance. In the fort, I was neither ostracized nor ill at ease—I was self-reliant, brave, ingeniously surviving, if lost.

Books are the other natural habitat for a child who loves words and adventures, and I was content when my parents read me *Moby-Dick, Pippi Longstocking,* or *The Hobbit.* I decided early that I would be a writer when I grew up. That, I thought, was the profession that went with the kind of woman I wanted to become: one who is free to do whatever she chooses.

I started keeping a diary in the third grade and, in solidarity with Anne Frank, I named it and personified it and made it my confidante. "The point that prompted me to keep a diary in the first place: I don't have a friend," Frank told Kitty, her journal. Writing is communicating with an unknown intimate who is always available, the way the faithful can turn to God. My lined notebooks were the only place I could say as much as I wanted, whenever I wanted. To this day I feel comforted and relieved of loneliness, no matter how foreign my surroundings, if I have a pad and a pen.

As a journalist, I've spent nearly two decades putting myself in foreign surroundings as frequently as possible. There is nothing I love more than traveling to a place where I know nobody, and where everything will be a surprise, and then writing about it. It's like having a new lover—even the parts you aren't crazy about have the crackling fascination of the unfamiliar.

The first story I ever published was about another world only an hour from my apartment. I was twenty-two, living in the East Village in a sixth-floor walk-up with a roommate and roaches, working as an assistant at *New York* magazine. My friend Mayita was an intern in the photo department who knew about a nightclub for obese women in Queens. We talked about it during our lunch break, when we were walking around midtown Manhattan with our plastic containers of limp salad, dreading going back to the office.

I was not a key member of the staff. It was my job to take the articles the writers faxed over and type them into the computer system—it was 1996, email was still viewed as a curious phenomenon that might blow over. Also, I had to input the crossword puzzle by looking back and forth between the paper the puzzle-crafter sent me and my computer screen, trying to remember if it went black, black, white, black, or black, white, black, black. I was in a constant state of embittered self-righteousness at the office. *How had I been mistaken for a charwoman?* Mayita was similarly horrified by the tumble her status had taken: As a senior at Wesleyan just a few months before, she had been the next Sally Mann. Now she alphabetized negatives all day. (When we expressed subdued versions of our outrage to our elders, their responses invariably included the phrase "paying your dues." It was not a phrase we cared for.)

We decided not to wait for someone at the office to give us permission to do what we really wanted. We took the subway about a million stops into Queens and went to a cavernous bar in Rego Park where women who weighed hundreds of pounds went to dance and flirt with their admirers and have lingerie pageants at four in the morning. It was very dark in there. The air smelled stagnant and sweaty and the drinks were so strong they fumed. But the women were magnificent, like enormous birds: feathery false eyelashes fluttering, tight, shiny dresses in peacock blue and canary yellow, the dim light reflecting off their sequins. Mayita and I stood out. We were puny, dressed in jeans and drab sweaters, little pigeons. It was scary, but electrifying: *What we're writing is more important than your anxiety and humiliation,* my competent self told me. So I went up to complete strangers with my notepad, and asked them to tell me their stories.

And they *did.* They told me about being fat little girls, or about how they got fat after they had children. They said they were sick of being ashamed, sick of apologizing for taking up so much space, so they'd come to believe that big was beautiful (or at least they'd come to believe it some of the time). They had passionate admirers, but it was difficult because they could never be sure if the men they dated—the "chubby chasers"—loved them for themselves, or for their fat. *For their fat!* I marveled on the way back to my apartment from the subway at 5 A.M. in the fading darkness.

The Manhattan around me in the late nineties was

glossy, greedy, hard. The slim women on Madison Avenue, on television, with their clicking heels and ironed-straight hair, gripped thousand-dollar handbags covered with interlocking G's. The restaurants people wanted to get into were sleek and ferociously expensive — nobody talked about *farm to table*; nobody wanted to see rough-hewn reclaimed wood. It was the genesis of Internet culture, and people my age kept making enormous sums of money on start-ups, on all sorts of things. A friend at work optioned the first big article she published at the magazine to a producer for half a million dollars when she was only twenty-five. (It was about the rich young publicists who maintained the city's nocturnal hierarchy, wielding their guest lists and their gift bags. "Most of us have as much power as older guys in suits," one of them said. "And soon enough we'll have more.")

There was no undercurrent of fear, very little pull against the prevailing tide of self-interest at that time. My generation had never experienced a real, prolonged war. Nobody thought about terrorism. Even climate change still seemed like something that could be safely ignored until the distant future — perhaps we would prevent it by recycling our soda cans. There was an unapologetic ethos of consumption in New York City, which the magazine I worked for both satirized and promoted. I found it alluring and alienating by turns.

So to locate an underworld of women who simply opted out of that slick culture, whose very bodies were unmistakable monuments of resistance, was thrilling. As I wrote my story (which turned out to be a lot harder than I'd imagined it would), I felt I was describing an exotic universe with its own aesthetic and manners, but even more, I was writing about an unconventional kind of female life. What does it mean to be a woman? What are the rules? What are your options and encumbrances? I wanted to tell stories that answered, or at least asked, those questions.

I was giddy when an editor at the magazine said that they would publish my article and Mayita's photos, and pay us for them. (They gave the story what is still the best headline I've ever had: WOMEN'S LB.) That article fee was special money, magic money—a reward for doing something that was its own reward. It was also two thousand dollars, which was more than my monthly take-home pay. Usually, it was a stretch to cover the cost of subway tokens and the rent on my grimy, depressing apartment. But after I got paid for my story, I went to the fancy salad bar at lunchtime for weeks. I took heedless scoops of the beets with blood-orange segments; I piled sliced steak next to them with abandon.

Writing was the solution to every problem—financial, emotional, intellectual. It had kept me company when I was a lonely child. It gave me an excuse to go places I would otherwise be unlikely to venture. It satisfied the edict my mother had issued many times throughout my life: "You have to make your own living; you never want to be dependent on a man." And it made me feel good, like there was a reason for me. "It is a very strange thing that people will give you a motor car if you will tell them a story," Virginia

Woolf said in an address to the National Society for Women's Service, a group of female professionals, in 1931. "It is a still stranger thing that there is nothing so delightful in the world as telling stories."

I'D BEEN PROMOTED TO staff writer by the time I fell in love, when I was twenty-eight. I got married a few years later—we all did. As we reached our thirtieth birthdays, my friends and I were like kernels of popcorn exploding in a pot: First one, then another, and pretty soon we were all bursting into matrimony. There were several years of peace, but then the pregnancies started popping. I found this unsettling.

To become a mother, I feared, was to relinquish your status as the protagonist of your own life. Your questions were answered, your freedom was gone, your path would calcify in front of you. And yet it still pulled at me. Being a professional explorer would become largely impossible if I had a child, but having a kid seemed in many ways like the wildest possible trip. Sometimes, on the long flights I took for my stories, I would listen to "Beginning of a Great Adventure," a Lou Reed song about impending parenthood: "A little me or he or she to fill up with my dreams," he sings. "A way of saying life is not a loss." As my friends, one after the next, made the journey from young woman to mother, it glared at me that I had not.

Some of my friends were outraged to discover that reproduction was not necessarily a simple mission. *Can you be-*

lieve I'm still not pregnant? they would ask, embittered, distraught, as their sex lives became suffused by grim determination, and they endured inseminations, in vitro, hormone injections, humiliation. *I've been trying for a year . . . two . . . five. I've spent six thousand dollars on these doctors . . . eight thousand . . . forty thousand.*

I listened to them. I said things that I hoped sounded comforting. But the thought in my head was always, *Of course.* It wasn't as though the research had just come in: Fertility wanes as the years accrue. We all knew this to be true. But somehow we imagined we could get around it.

We lived in a world where we had control of so much. If we didn't want to carry groceries up the steps, we ordered them online and waited in our sweatpants on the fourth floor for a man from Asia or Latin America to come panting up, encumbered with our cat litter and organic bananas. If we wanted to communicate with one another when we were on opposite ends of the earth, we picked up devices that didn't exist when we were young and sent each other texts, emails, pictures we'd taken seconds earlier without any film. Anything seemed possible if you had ingenuity, money, and tenacity. But the body doesn't play by those rules.

We were raised to think we could do what we wanted—we were free to be you and me! And many of our parents' revolutionary dreams had actually come true. A black man really could be president. It was sort of okay to be gay—gay married, even. You could be female and have an engrossing career and you didn't have to be a wife or mother (although, let's face it, it still seemed advisable: Spinsterhood never exactly lost its taint). Sometimes our parents were dazzled by the sense of possibility they'd bestowed upon us. Other times, they were aghast to recognize their own entitlement, staring back at them magnified in the mirror of their off-spring.

Daring to think that the rules do not apply is the mark of a visionary. It's also a symptom of narcissism.

I ALWAYS GET TERRIFIED before I travel. I become convinced that this time I won't be able to figure out the map, or communicate with non-English-speakers, or find the people I need in order to write the story I've been sent in search of. I will be lost and incompetent and vulnerable.

So it was with childbearing: I was afraid for almost a decade. I didn't like childhood, and I was afraid that I'd have a child who didn't, either. I was afraid I would be an awful mother. And I was afraid of being grounded, sessile—stuck in one spot for twenty years of oboe lessons and math homework that I hadn't been able to finish the first time around.

I paid attention to what I saw and read on the subject. "A child, yes, is a vortex of anxieties," Elena Ferrante wrote in her novel *The Lost Daughter.* Her protagonist eventually rips herself away from her children, and enters an experience of the sublime: "Everything starting from zero. No habit, no sensations dulled by predictability. I was I, I produced thoughts not distracted by any concern other than the tangled thread of dreams and desires." If you held a baby all night and day, your hands would not be free to cling to that tangled thread.

I once saw an interview with Joni Mitchell in which she explained why she didn't marry Graham Nash and have his babies when they were a couple in the sixties. She turned her back on the domestic dream she had inspired him to canonize: "I'll light the fire, you place the flowers in the vase." After he proposed, Mitchell found herself thinking about her grandmother, a frustrated musician who felt so trapped by motherhood and women's work that one afternoon she "kicked the kitchen door off the hinges." Her life would not be about self-expression. She resigned herself to her reality.

Mitchell thought that she would end up like her grandmother if she chose family and domesticity. So instead, as she sang in "Don Juan's Reckless Daughter," she went roaming, "out on the vast and subtle plains of mystery."

I wanted to meet those mysteries, too. I wanted to feel the limitless Mongolian steppe spread out in front of me. I wanted to know what it smells like in the morning in Rajasthan. Why? "I want to do it because I want to do it," Amelia Earhart once wrote in a letter to her husband. "Women must try to do things as men have tried."

I would not kick the door off its hinges. I would not choose the muffling comforts of home. I would be the explorer, not the mummy.

2

THE NIGHT BEFORE I LEFT, AFRICA WAS GOLDEN AND pulsating in my mind. I imagined myself with pad in hand, furiously taking notes under a red sun. I would be fearless, in love with my work and the wide world. I would fall into bed at night exhilarated, my mind zooming with thought.

I was thirty-five years old and flying to Johannesburg to report the most ambitious story of my career. Over the course of a dozen years on the job, I'd grown accustomed to writing certain kinds of articles: compact profiles of public figures; essays about pop culture. This was something else. Everything I'd done before seemed like practice, preparation. This felt like the beginning of my adult life as a writer.

There was a runner from Limpopo, a rural region of South Africa on the borders of Botswana, Mozambique, and Zimbabwe, whose picture I had seen in the paper and could not look away from. Her name was Caster Semenya. She had grown up in a remote village of small brick houses and sun-baked mud-and-dung huts, running barefoot with a track team that could not afford sneakers. She came from a place where few people had cars or indoor plumbing or opportunities for greatness, and she had kept on running until she was powerful and unstoppable. Semenya had been recruited by the University of Pretoria and, at eighteen, she had just won the 2009 World Championships in Berlin, setting a new national record for her event. She seemed destined for the Olympics.

But the other runners didn't think it was fair. "For me, she is not a woman. She is a man," said the Italian runner Elisa Cusma, who had come in sixth in Berlin. "These kind of people should not run with us."

"Just look at her," said the Russian who had finished fifth.

Semenya was breathtakingly butch. She had a strong jawline and a build that slid straight from her ribs to her hips; her torso was like the breastplate on a suit of armor. Even before she left Pretoria, there had been gossip about her appearance. In response, the International Association of Athletics Federations, the organization that governs Semenya's sport, instructed her to undergo "gender testing": she was taken to a doctor for an inspection of her genitals and given a blood test to measure her testosterone level. She was told she was being tested for doping, but she knew that this was something else, though she couldn't say what. Like most people in her village, Semenya had never been to a gynecologist before.

In Berlin, Semenya saw a report on television that her

test results had been leaked, and that they showed she had three times the amount of testosterone found in average females, possibly because she had been born with undescended testes instead of ovaries. They called her a hermaphrodite—a word she'd never heard. "We live by simple rules," as her father put it later. "I don't know what a chromosome is." The story became an international tabloid sensation.

Semenya's countrymen were appalled by the idea of a person who thought she was one thing suddenly being told that she was something else: The classification and reclassification of human beings has a haunted history in South Africa. When Semenya returned to Johannesburg, thousands of supporters waited to cheer her at O. R. Tambo International Airport. Nelson Mandela and President Jacob Zuma made a point of meeting her to offer their congratulations. People were outraged that a teenager had been examined and analyzed, like the Hottentot Venus before her, by European men who were fascinated by her exotic, anomalous appearance.

The truth is, I was fascinated, too. It was a story that made you question the meaning of gender: What makes a person female? A vagina? A womb? A chromosome? (What if someone has two out of three?) What, in the end, is a woman?

I convinced my editor to send me to South Africa, though I'd never written a real story in a foreign country before. I had no idea how I would find Semenya, who certainly didn't have a publicist or a website. I didn't know how to reach the athletic officials who were scandalizing her country with their mismanagement of the situation, or the politicians who were using it to foment populist rage. In fact, when I boarded the plane in New York, I did not have a single contact in Africa.

That had seemed like a mere detail the night before I left. But somewhere over the Atlantic, it became a crisis. *What* had I been thinking? I had entertained visions of sitting down in the bleachers at the University of Pretoria, where Semenya was a freshman, and looking up to find her speeding around the track. (Perhaps next I would pursue a story on the surviving Beatles by flying to London and waiting for them at the crosswalk on Abbey Road?) I tried to calm myself: *We'll just figure it out; this isn't quantum physics.* But I found myself unconvincing.

I had finally pushed it too far. I would be punished for my hubris with failure. Africa, so glorious and promising the night before, grew menacing in my mind. I thought of our safe, friendly house on Shelter Island, with its open windows and quilts folded in the linen closet, and I wished that I had never left.

BUT SOMEHOW, IF YOU want to badly enough, you can always report a story. It feels like magic but it works like carpentry. You build a frame, and then you build on that, and pretty soon you have something to stand on so you can hammer away at a height that was initially out of reach. You start by contacting people who are easy to find, even if they are only tangentially related to your subject. My first call when I got to South Africa was to the student council president at the University of Pretoria. He led me to the head of athletics, a big white man with a bushy mustache and a strong Afrikaans accent, who introduced me to Semenya's trainer. Her trainer led me to her first coach, a bald black man with rheumy eyes named Phineas Sako, whom I met on a dirt road in the middle of Limpopo, where he had gathered twenty teenage athletes for running practice.

Over the sound of the wind, I could hear music coming from a brick-front bar down the road, and chickens squawking in front yards, where they were kept in enclosures made out of tree branches. Most of the young runners in the Moletjie Athletics Club had walked at least half an hour from their villages to get to the meeting place. Practice for the sprinters was on a nearby track, where donkeys and goats were grazing on the sprouting spring grass. For cross-country, they trained in the miles of bush that spread out toward the mountains in the distance, but the land was webbed with brambles, and the thorns were a serious problem for the athletes, who ran barefoot. "We can't stop and say we don't have running shoes, because we don't have money, the parents don't have money," Sako said. "So what must we do? We just go on."

Joyce, a tiny girl in a pink sweater who was eighteen but looked about twelve, told me, "I want to be the world champion." Her voice was so soft it was almost a whisper. "I *will* be the world champion. Caster is making me proud."

Sako said that Semenya had always been an extraordinary runner. "I used to tell Caster that she must try her level best," he said. "By performing the best, maybe good guys with big stomachs full of money will see her and help her with schooling and the likes. That is the motivation. And she *always* tried her level best."

But throughout her childhood, her gender had been the subject of suspicion and curiosity wherever she went. "'It looks like a boy'—that's the right words," Sako told me. "They used to say, 'It looks like a boy.'" Semenya became accustomed to visiting the bathroom with a member of a competing team so that they could look at her private parts and then get on with the race. "They are doubting me," she would explain to her coach, as she headed off the field toward the lavatory again.

After I had interviewed Sako's runners, I gave him a ride home in my rental car on the dirt road that split the endless dry, golden bush. It became clear he had skepticism of his own—about my womanhood. He did not understand what I was doing in Limpopo. "Where are your children?" he wanted to know. When I told him that I didn't have any, he shook his head in disbelief.

I tried to say that writing for me was like running for Caster Semenya: the thing I had to do. But Sako was still shaking his head when he got out of the car. "You Americans," he said. "You know nothing."

———

I WENT TO CAPE TOWN NEXT. A soft-spoken Ethiopian man named Zerihun picked me up at the airport. On the way to the hotel he told me about his wife, with whom he'd come to Cape Town seven years earlier; she loved the new landscape, the spiky greens and yellows of the fynbos plants. I told him about my article and all the people I had to find and he said that we would do it together—he would drive me everywhere, we would be a team of foreigners.

I stayed at the foot of the Bo-Kaap, the Cape Malay neighborhood where candy-colored houses crawl up the steep slope toward Signal Hill. I felt an uncanny sense of recognition when I got to town, something like the way you feel when you meet a new person whom you instantly know will be important to you. My closest friend, Emma, is the child of two Jewish South African émigrés, and I could hear the familiar cadence of her parents' speech all around me. Expressions that I'd assumed were particular to her family turned out to be national turns of phrase. "Shame," the woman behind the front desk at the Cape Heritage Hotel said with compassion when I mentioned I'd accidentally left my sneakers behind in Pretoria, just as Emma or her mom would say, "Shame," if you stubbed your toe. Sentences often ended with "hey?"—a beguiling appeal for concord, as in "Semenya's just a kid, hey?" I smiled every time I heard it, thinking of Emma in college: "This party stinks, hey? Let's go home already."

Zerihun and I were both nervous that we would get lost driving through Khayelitsha, a massive township on the outskirts of the city, where shacks made of corrugated tin and wooden boards sprawl for miles along mostly unmarked dirt roads, punctuated by beauty parlors and fruit stands in structures no bigger than telephone booths. But we had no trouble finding the solid brick house of an LGBT activist named Funeka Soldaat. She was a boisterous woman with a shaved head who spoke to me for hours with fearless warmth about the gender politics of black South Africa. She was joyful, even though she was on her way to court later that day to listen to the proceedings against several men accused of raping and murdering a lesbian in her neighborhood. "They are raping lesbians to 'correct' them," she said. "In order that they can be a 'proper woman.'" It was something she had experienced herself.

There was no leeway for a woman to deviate from the expectations of her gender, Soldaat said. Her differences would be either eliminated or ignored. Soldaat was responding, in part, to a public statement by a politician named Julius Malema, the head of the African National Congress's radical, powerful Youth League, who had said he would "never accept the categorization of Caster Semenya as a hermaphrodite, because in South Africa and the entire world of sanity, such does not exist." Malema had tried to frame the notion as an unwelcome Western import: "Don't impose your hermaphrodite concepts on us."

But South Africa has among the highest rates of intersex

births in the world, though nobody knows why. Soldaat had a cousin, she said, "just like Caster: She don't have breasts. She never get a period. Everybody thinks she's a guy. We call them in Xhosa *italisi.*" It was a whispered term. "One thing that is so difficult for African people," Soldaat continued, "there's no way that you can discuss something that's happened below the belt." It pained her to imagine Semenya in Germany, puzzling through the reports on television, alone. "All the time you don't know what is happening in your body. And there's nobody that try to explain to you."

BACK IN MY ROOM, with my notepads spread out on the big four-poster bed and the brilliant colors of Cape Town flashing outside the open window, I transcribed my recordings on my laptop. The opportunity in front of me made it difficult to sit still. This story had everything: a faraway place with its own taxonomy and atmosphere, the smell of wood smoke and dope blowing through the township, the hadeda ibises floating prehistorically through the pink sky. And at the center of it was a woman who was too strong, too powerful—*too much.*

I told everybody I met who knew Semenya that I wanted to interview her and asked them to help me plead my case. But a wall of lawyers had sprung up around her now, deflecting grotty tabloid requests from all over the world. And to Semenya herself, no doubt, reporters were the enemy, the people who had humiliated her in front of the eyes of the world at the very moment of triumph she had been working toward her entire life. I still wanted to be in her presence, however briefly, just to shake her hand and hear her voice. I wished we could have even a momentary encounter.

One morning, when I was back in Pretoria getting ready to interview an administrator at the university, I had the thought, *I'm going to meet Caster Semenya today.* I laughed at myself an hour later as I sat in the bleachers, killing time before my appointment. I was surrounded by a spread of neatly partitioned fields, as in a Bruegel painting, the land worked by athletes instead of farmers. Runners in little packs cruised past me into the distance. Spring sunlight flicked along the blue surface of the swimming pool.

A figure in a black sweatshirt with the hood up walked along the path about thirty yards in front of me. There was something about this person's build and movements that drew my attention. I got up and followed along the path, until I caught up to the person behind the cafeteria, talking to a waiter and a cook, both of whom were much shorter than she was. It was Caster Semenya. She didn't look like a teenage girl, or a teenage boy. She looked like something else, something magnificent.

I told her I had come from New York City to write about her, and she asked me why. "Because you're the champion," I said.

She snorted and said, "You make me laugh."

I asked her if she would talk to me, not about the tests,

but about her evolution as an athlete, her progression from Limpopo to the world stage. She shook her head vigorously. "No," she said. "I can't talk to you. I can't talk to anyone. I can't say to anyone how I feel or what's in my mind."

I said I thought that must suck.

"No," she said firmly. Her voice was strong and low. "It sucks when I was running and they were writing those things. That is when it sucks. Now I just have to walk away. That's all I can do." She made a very small, bemused smile. "Walk away from all of this, maybe forever." Then she took a few steps backward, turned around, and did.

I had found the person I'd come looking for. At that moment, I felt for the first time that I could trust myself to attempt whatever I felt compelled to do as a reporter. It was time to go home.

BUT AS I PACKED my suitcase at the Cape Heritage, it occurred to me that I should take this chance to see some of Africa's wildlife. Who knew when—or if—I'd ever be back in this part of the world? I did not, after all, have children. I was free to experience just a little more.

I decided I would spend a weekend in the Kruger National Park. I was eager to see the copper herds of impala, the leopards winding themselves in the trees. I imagined my fellow tourists would be like Robert Redford and Meryl Streep in Out of Africa—daring loners. Instead, they were suburban couples from England and Australia on romantic vacations. At mealtimes, I wrote in my journal or read *Disgrace*, while the husbands and wives, boyfriends and girlfriends, sat at their tables laughing and drinking wine. Every evening, the staff placed rose petals in the shape of a heart on all the beds and I brushed them off into the trash. I was very lonesome in the dark.

I loved the early mornings, though, sitting in the back of a Land Rover in the last of the darkness while the guide told us how to identify rhinoceros dung. The sky brightened. The leaves shook, and what at first seemed to be the shadowy gray of a tree trunk would become an elephant.

On the day that I first saw a pride of lions flopping on their backs in the dry yellow grass and licking each other so tenderly it was hard not to jump out of the vehicle to pet them, I made the mistake that would lead to my first real regret. Up until then, my regrets had been feathery things, the regrets of a privileged child. (*I should have gone on semester abroad. I should have lost my virginity to someone nice.*) But on that morning, I made the first of many real mistakes that would stack up on top of one another until they blocked out the sun.

I did not get mauled by an animal. I had not been mugged or assaulted in dangerous Johannesburg. I had not even failed at the unlikely task I had invented for myself when I insisted I could find my way and my story on another continent about which I knew nothing. The world had left me unscathed.

But the danger that we invite into our lives can come in

the most unthreatening shape, the most pedestrian: the cellphone you press against your head, transmitting the voice of your mother, pouring radiation into your brain day after day; the little tick bite in the garden that leaves you aching and palsied for years. It can come in the form of an email from an old lover whom you have not spoken with for many years, which you receive when you are back at the lodge, sitting under a thatched roof drinking a cup of milky tea. It can come when, instead of writing to the person with whom you share a home and a history, the person you adore and have married, you write to your old lover. And you say, "Today I saw a family of lions licking each other in the yellow grass, and they looked like they were in love."

3

MY MOTHER KNEW INSTINCTIVELY THAT DANGER COULD come in a friendly box from the grocery store, full of brightly colored cereal that gets inside your body and rots you quietly from the inside out. She had inherited from her own mother the immigrant's mistrust for authority, and combined it with insurrectionary tendencies left over from her days as a student radical, and what it all added up to in the kitchen was a ban on Cheez Doodles. In the house where I grew up, in clean, leafy Westchester, nothing was artificially colored. Hot dogs were verboten. It wasn't spartan: There were always apples and bananas in a blue bowl; there were Cheddar and Jarlsberg in the cheese drawer. There were all the ingredients you needed to make white bean soup from the *Moosewood Cookbook*. For a time, I think my mother really believed in right living through tofu.

I remember my maternal grandmother teaching me to make cheese blintzes when I was about eleven, an actual lesson: how much to beat the batter with a fork (until it's frothy); when to pull the pancake out of the skillet (when the edge becomes a light-brown lace); and how to fold the filling inside (like a present that you fry). But mostly I learned to cook from my mother. There weren't any blintz-style lessons. I absorbed her preferences and prejudices over the years the way that I absorbed her gestures and her speech pattern, until ultimately my cooking tastes slightly but unmistakably like hers. I sat around our Mexican-tiled kitchen and learned to love making pies, and to be vexed by other people's dirty dishes, and to believe that if there is no salad, there is no meal. I don't remember my mother telling me to stick a half a lemon inside the cavity of a chicken before you roast it, but I know that's what you do. Or I know that's what she did.

As far as I could tell, there were two modes of cooking: festive and obligatory. My mother prepared obligatory dinners for my father and me every night when she came home from work at the daycare center she had started in the local public school system. She attended a women's consciousness-raising group for two decades—wearing sneakers or flat sandals, no jewelry, her dark, curly hair fluffy and free—but my mother did the cooking in our family, even when my father was between jobs. In regular rotation were meatloaf (not her best work, and consequently something I never make), a lovely pan-fried chicken breast dipped in breadcrumbs mixed with Parmesan cheese, and my favorite, noodle kugel with golden raisins, which is really more of a dessert if you're honest about it.

There was a corresponding orbit of moods this obligatory food preparation induced in my mother: no-nonsense competence, spunky pride, and seething resentment. From my mother, I learned that you can make your family feel a wonderful sense of protected indulgence by cooking them something with jolly care. I also learned that you can launch a powerful campaign of resistance by mincing garlic like a martyr.

My mother's festive cookery was really something. Her repertoire magically expanded on special occasions, and she busted out with impressive roasts, time-consuming cheesecakes, and gleaming cornbread. She always managed to make enough food for the eight or ten or twelve guests who materialized. (Which to me is still amazing. When I triple or quintuple a recipe, I rarely just get more of it. I usually get something weird.) Then she set the table with blue spatterware and the blue-rimmed glasses my parents had schlepped home in bubble wrap from a vacation in the Yucatán along with the kitchen tiles, transforming our pigpen of a dining room into a snappy café.

There was another dimension of festive food preparation in my house. My mother had a friend, a special friend, who visited regularly. His name was Marcus. He lived with his wife and their two sons in Albany, where he worked as the administrator of a mental health facility. A very tall, handsome black man, Marcus had graying hair and a gut about the size and hardness of a bowling ball by the time I knew him, but when my mother—and father—met him at the University of Wisconsin–Madison in the late sixties, I bet he was almost majestic. He was a basketball player then, already divorced from his first wife, whom he had left with two children in the South. (He rarely saw them and never spoke of them.) He and my mother had been involved on and off in college. Eventually she married my father, a history grad student from the Bronx who was funny, Jewish, and, at five feet three, even shorter than their only child would grow up to be. But my mother and this other, much taller man stayed in touch.

When Marcus visited, my mother whipped out the Mexican glasses. She made her cornbread. She grew giddy and animated and did not complain, in word or gesture, about clearing the plates after her family and her guest had eaten the meal she'd just prepared. Then we would go to the living room and sit on the blue couches, and Cat Stevens would sing on the record player, "I have my freedom / I can make my own rules."

Marcus brought treats. He brought pot, which he grew in his backyard, and my parents would close the curtains and smoke it with him before consuming the rest of his offerings. He brought apricots dipped in chocolate. He brought pigs' trotters in glass jars, which were never touched by the diminutive Jews in his company. Once or twice, he brought incredible cinnamon buns from the Ovens of Brittany in Madison, which he must have had shipped. He was a cloud of hedonism blowing into our household—which usually gloried in its own imaginary deprivation (in contrast to the indulgences all around us: Larchmont with its Lexuses). With Marcus's coming, the rules and the ambiance and the cuisine changed. One night, it was determined that the best ribs in the world were in Philadelphia, so that is where we went. I remember sitting in the backseat of a taxi, hurtling out of 30th Street Station toward the Rib Crib, panicked. Events that would have been adventures with just my parents took on a different tone when Marcus was around.

When he came to visit, Marcus slept on a pile of blankets my mother carefully arranged on the TV-room floor next to the brown corduroy couch. But it was clear to me, from as early as I can remember anything, that his presence represented a grave threat to my father and me. Marcus had the power to change my mother from a stern regulator of all food containing sugar into a giggling nymph pouring giant glasses of 7UP, as carefree as if it were carrot juice. It was terrifying to see her so happy. When Marcus wasn't at our house, he called frequently, and my mother would go into my parents' bedroom with the phone and close the door and I would try to think of reasons to pound on it. She would go visit him, too, or they'd meet in Saratoga, where they bet on the horses. I was acutely aware of the possibility that someday, when she drove off in our rusted green station wagon, she might never come back.

Sometimes she brought us with her. There were Christmases at Marcus's house in Albany, where the food was outrageously unwholesome and delicious—fried chicken, brownies, every kind of soda. He gave lavish gifts. His sons got Ataris and Dungeons & Dragons stuff and I got intricate, expensive furniture for my dollhouse. He gave my father a beautiful brown leather briefcase and the softest suede jacket I'd ever seen in Marcus's favorite rusty shade. (Marcus was color-blind, and this reddish brown, I think, was what every color looked like to him.) A few days later, we'd drive home through the grimy snow and eat leftovers. My mother would seem deflated and my father would be short-tempered and gruff, prone to blowups over the strangest things.

As I got older, I badgered my mother many times for the truth about her relationship with Marcus. There was something wrong with it, but what? Wasn't my mother entitled to have a close—even a "special"—friend? Shouldn't her friend, like my friends, be allowed to sleep over?

When I first learned about sex, I was excited because it seemed like something that could prove useful for quantifying betrayal. Sex! With this one new idea, I had my whole case: If you were married, then you were only ever allowed to have sex with your spouse. (Why? Who knew. But those were the rules.) So if my mother was having *sex* with Marcus, then that was bad, open-and-shut. The problem was proving it, and I came up with only one not-very-effective strategy for that: I asked my mother.

ME

    Do you have sex with Marcus?

MOM

    Marcus sleeps in the TV room.

ME

    Did you used to have sex with Marcus?

MOM

    Marcus and I have always had a
    special connection.

She would grow defensive and I would get bewildered. Battering my mother with questions and accusations did not make me feel good. I felt cruel, abusive, but also paranoid, hysterical. It was as if I were a little girl again, afraid of shadows in the stucco walls of our hallway; they looked like monsters—*were* monsters, to me in my rigid insomniac sentinel. But you can never tell with shadows. You have to be vigilant, always, because maybe you're crazy, but maybe you're right.

I went to bed with the lights on every night as a child. It was fine as long as I could hear the muffled sounds of Johnny Carson on television down the hall. But after my parents had gone to sleep and the house went silent I came unhinged—turned into a cat tensed to bolt under the furniture at the sound of a footfall. What was familiar became fearsome. The walls that had been inert all day were possessed at night, vibrating with menace. I sat erect, struggling to keep my eyes open until sunrise, when safety was restored and I could sleep for a few ragged hours before school. My parents took me to see a child psychologist; I remember cutting pancakes out of construction paper in his office. He let me pour mucilage all over them, golden brown and viscous, perfectly maple syrup–like. It was nothing serious, he told them. Their daughter was just sensitive, overwhelmed by her perception of a world that seemed unstable.

I had been sleeping through the night—untormented, in the dark—for just a few years when my father moved to Washington, D.C., to take a job. For years, he'd written copy for a small company that did development work for various lefty causes—the antinuclear movement, the NAACP, Greenpeace. He would sit on the corduroy couch after dinner rewriting sentences on lined yellow pads, tapping a pencil against his mustache, and sometimes sighing and mumbling, "All right already," when he finally got it right. That ended abruptly when my father got in a fight with his boss and told him to go fuck himself. A tense period of yellow-pad-free unemployment followed. ("See?" my mother said. "You never want to be dependent on a man. You *have* to make your own living.") Then, when I was twelve, my father accepted a position at the National Abortion Rights Action League. It gradually became clear that we were not going to follow him to Washington once he settled in, as had been promised.

———

WHEN I WAS FOURTEEN, I had a shaggy sixteen-year-old boyfriend named Josh with whom I felt a desperate, precarious intimacy. Both of our homes were like embassies of the 1960s in the manicured foreign terrain of Reagan-era suburbia. Neither of our mothers wore makeup. Both of our sets of parents were sluggishly but obviously parting, and Joshua and I were paradoxically determined to assert our independence from them by mimicking the very expressions of rebellion they had taught us. We listened to Neil Young and Bob Dylan. We draped our beds with batik. We read *On the Road* and *The Prophet* and the poetry of Robert Creeley. When Josh and I started going out, I felt that I had been delivered from my isolation, my uncoolness, and my family. It did not occur to me that I got the ideas for my outfits from photographs of my mother taken at a time when she looked happy to be with my father.

Josh and I smoked pot whenever we could get it, and, one night at the Capitol Theatre in Port Chester, where we had come to see a band named after a song by the Grateful Dead, Josh and I ate little paper tabs of LSD. Panic set in quickly. I was desperate to go home, but once I got there the walls were swarming with monstrous faces, as they had throughout my girlhood, but now they were *moving*. Everything in my field of vision was moving—furniture and doorways fragmenting into squares that pulsated around one another: *tick, tick, tick, tick, tick!* I was convinced that I could hear the breathing of dead people deep in the ground.

The horrors of my childhood were not, as it had recently seemed, the irrational—the amusing!—fears of an innocent. I had been right all along: The world was ugly and terrifying, nothing made sense, and, worst of all, I was alone in perceiving the truth. I had flashbacks for years. I was an insomniac well into my twenties.

I WAS OFTEN EXHAUSTED growing up, but I was very well nourished. Every day, my mother packed me a well-balanced lunch to take to school, until my teenage years, when I was too angry to allow her the satisfaction of doing that single thing right. Marcus came even more frequently after my father's departure, and my distrust of him metastasized into loathing. Everything he brought that seemed good was bad for you. I had a brief but vocal flirtation with vegetarianism.

When I graduated from high school, my mother issued a proclamation: The kitchen is closed. She had delivered me healthy to a college with a cafeteria; her work was complete. There would be no more flank steak with Vidalia onions marinated in red wine, as there had been in the eighties, when my parents had friends over for long nights that began with crudités and dill dip and ended with Frusen Glädjé and marijuana. There would be no more dubious pasta creations, of the sort my mother favored after my father moved to Washington and she began asserting a preference for rustic furniture made of pale wood. (My father, left to his own devices, went immoderately Art Deco and rekindled an almost-forgotten love for Marlboro Lights. His apartment on Connecticut Avenue was as dark and smoky as an opium den on the Left Bank, circa 1930.)

Not long after my mother closed the kitchen and ceased both festive and obligatory cooking, she ended her relationships with both of the men she'd been feeding since her early twenties. My parents got around to legally divorcing just before I graduated from college, and during that same period, my mother stopped going on trips with Marcus. She stopped taking his calls. She ceased stocking his soda and lost interest in red meat, then chicken, and finally she gave up her greatest love, lobster. Marcus had only worked as a side dish.

My mother had become someone else—someone who didn't need a man, let alone two. Someone who didn't cook.

For several years, she ate nothing but frozen yogurt, toast, and takeout. She became a Shiatsu masseuse. When I visited, my mother would say, "Let's get Chinese!" and then she would order spring rolls, Buddha's Delight, and wok-fried baby bok choy. She went on an extended trip to Asia, where she drank yak butter tea in Tibet and saw the ancient terra-cotta warriors of Shaanxi. "It's amazing," she told me when she got back. "These people get to wear paja-

dicted for embezzling from the mental hospitals he ran. And that he'd been convicted of assaulting a pizza delivery-man. My mother mentioned that once, before I was born, he had tried to strangle her.

After my mother settled into life on Cape Cod, she started hosting Thanksgiving and making sensational tur-keys that she didn't eat because she never returned to meat, white or red. Instead, she would pack the leftovers in Tupperware and freeze the gravy in ice cube trays. Then she'd stick all of that in a cooler with ice packs and hand it to me triumphantly when I got in the car to leave. She was victorious on fronts culinary and parental: She had pro-duced a daughter who was an adequate cook and a valiant eater. And who wasn't dependent on a man.

mas and eat Chinese food every single day!" I pointed o\
that she had pretty much just described her own life.

Then one day, on a whim, my mother moved to Cape
Cod, after she saw a house she liked there with an apple
tree in the backyard. She had never been fully comfortable
in Larchmont—the houses were too close together, the
women were too polished. In this new house, in this place
of beaches and blueberry bushes, her kitchen provisionally
reopened. She started making omelets. Next came the occasional soup. Lobster, naturally, was reintroduced to her
diet. Eventually, she took up with Ed, a local man who
makes eggplant parmigiana and mushroom caps with
breadcrumbs, and whose worst fault as a human being is
that he uses powdered garlic. They've been a couple for
nearly a decade, but they live in their own homes, ten minutes away from each other; they do their cooking in separate
kitchens.

My father remarried when I was in my twenties, to a
gregarious woman with red hair from the South named Jennie Lee, who gave me an amazing recipe for pork tender-
loin and a set of green Depression glass dishes on which to
serve it. (You marinate the meat overnight in equal parts
orange juice and soy sauce with a few smashed garlic cloves,
some brown sugar, and a teaspoon of ginger. Then you put
it in the broiler for twelve minutes on each side, and smear
apricot preserves all over it while it's cooling—people think
it's a complicated glaze and get very impressed.)

A few years ago, we heard that Marcus was being in-

4

AFTER MY STORY ABOUT THE OBESE WOMEN'S NIGHTCLUB was published in *New York,* people there paid slightly more attention to me. But I remained a lackey and I burned with the desire to rise. I hurled myself up Madison Avenue from the subway station toward our office every morning muttering to myself, obsessed with *becoming.* I was scrappy and I was greedy, but with an edge of desperation like a hungry cat.

I met an editor named John Homans my first week at the magazine. I went out one morning to what we called the Bat Cave, a fire escape in a dark airshaft off the side of the office, where people went to sneak cigarettes under the dripping hot-water pipes. There was space enough for only two people to stand quite close together, and Homans was already out there, puffing away, looking like Harrison Ford's younger brother. He was thirty-five; I must have been twenty-one. I told him my name and said that I knew I should know who he was, but I didn't. "There's no reason you should know who I am," he said, which turned out not to be at all true.

He edited all of the best writers at the magazine. If Homans decided to shine his light on you, your byline would appear on the cover, your assignments would be actual stories—interesting, complicated, not the vulgar stuff we sometimes ran about plastic surgeons and real estate in the Hamptons. Much more important, if Homans worked with you, it meant that you were good, or would be by the time he was done with you. It meant you were going to be a real writer.

It took years to ingratiate myself. I would look for excuses to loiter around his office—an imaginary fax that needed sending, a visit to the other underlings who sat outside his door—so I could listen to him yell at his writers on the phone: "When are you going to file that fucking thing?" Or, if they reported a good detail, "Ha! Can you imagine?" As the months inched by, he grew friendlier in his gruff New England way. "It's a big shit sandwich and everybody has to take a bite," he'd tell me, when I would complain about having to write blurbs about exterminators or car services.

When I was very little, before we moved to Westchester, my family lived on the second floor of a row house in the Bronx; in my memory, our block looked exactly like Sesame Street. There was a teenage boy across the street named Neil Reardon, whom I worshipped. I wanted to dress like him. I wanted to pee standing up because I somehow knew that he did. My mother and I would sit out on our front stoop, and when I saw him emerge from his house, I would tug on her sleeve so that she would get up and we could move closer to him. It was toddler love: reverential, subordinate, romantic but not strictly sexual. I wanted to impress him and be him. I would stare up at his sixteen-year-old head and swoon at his tall, Gentile dynamism.

That's how I felt about John Homans. It took me nearly seven years to come up with a story that actually interested him. I noticed that strippers and porn stars and their aesthetic were weirdly and suddenly everywhere. On my way to work in the morning, I passed an enormous billboard picturing Jenna Jameson, the highest-earning porn star in the world at the time, who had a book on the bestseller list. There were pole-dancing classes at my gym. Teenagers were wearing Playboy Bunny T-shirts. Thongs became a thing. And bizarrely, the lingo that went with this look was borrowed from the women's movement: If you saw a push-up bra, you knew you were seconds away from hearing the word "empowerment." I would write about this. I would make up a name for it. I would come up with an explanation!

"That'll be fun for you, Miss Ari," Homans told me in his usual detached, vaguely ironic tone. But I could tell by the way he was wiggling his fingers in the air, playing an invisible stand-up bass, that I had aroused his enthusiasm.

It took forever to write the thing. Usually, you find out about a story, you go report it, and then you come up with an idea about what you've learned, a narrative to organize the information. But this was a story about an idea, and I had to find situations and people that were illustrative. I was very much a beginner. Some of *New York*'s best stories by the writers I most respected had identified cultural phenomena and given them names they could never shake. (Tom Wolfe's "Radical Chic.") But you need confidence and wide-ranging knowledge to write an essay like that, and you need real style to distract your reader through the iffy patches in your argument. I didn't have any of that.

So I worked by trial and error. I wrote draft after draft and Homans told me what he thought I meant—which tended to be more interesting than what I actually meant—and he showed me the difference between that and what I'd put on the page. When the essay was finished, it was not the masterpiece I'd intended. It wasn't even a cover story. But it was enough to convince Homans we ought to do another story together, and then another.

Eventually, that essay would become my first book. But securing Homans's attention was more meaningful to me. A real editor isn't just someone you work with; he's your guide. He sees your brain doing its thing and learns its weaknesses and abilities, and if he's really good, he figures out what you need to hear to compensate for the former and accentuate the latter. He is the person you trust with the most intimate thing you have, your own voice.

Often, that trust infects the entire relationship. There is very little that went on in my life during my twenties and early thirties that I did not tell Homans about; for years he weighed in on every decision I made.

I WENT OUT ALMOST every night during that period, trying to figure out who I should be and be with. There was a comedian who had a show on cable about staying out late and going to dive bars across the country after his sets—we went to them together when he was home in New York. Not long after September 11, when the air in the city still stank of scorched plastic and flamed-out fuel, we drank whiskey at the Stoned Crow, a sticky, subterranean place near Washington Square Park with initials and obscenities carved into the walls. It was just a few blocks away from the corner where I had watched with my neighbors as the first tower fell out of the sky.

The day after it happened, there were army tanks all along Fourteenth Street and I remember a group of young men in a pickup truck driving slowly past, holding up American flags and a banner on which they'd written RE-VENGE. You had to show the police your ID to get onto your street if you lived downtown; anthrax started showing up in the mail, mostly addressed to members of the press. Sikh cabdrivers were getting assaulted because people thought they looked like Osama bin Laden. Hundreds of photos of missing people hung in Grand Central Terminal and along a chain-link fence on Greenwich Street near Saint Vincent's Hospital, which had mobilized for an influx of victims after the attacks. But the people were gone. The skyscrapers that had been the Southern Cross of Manhattan, gone.

That night at the bar, the comedian told me that this was to be our generation's test, our Great War. He sounded fleetingly and poignantly heroic—I was used to him kidding about everything. (I loved his jokes, which were vulgar and absurd: "A guy, let's call him me, was fucking the left eye of a pumpkin. If that pumpkin didn't want it why was it smiling at me?") He reminded me of my rough maternal grandfather, a tough Jew. The comedian felt achingly familiar, the brown-eyed husband some part of me always expected to have. It pained me not to be with him but I pushed him away all the same.

Before him, there was a blond boy who looked at me with a covetous lust that elated me. I met him just after my father was diagnosed with cancer. It was the same week I dropped an air conditioner out the window at my friend's apartment on St. Marks Place. The grimy, wet summer heat was heavy in her living room, and it was back when we were so unbelievably young that we not only smoked cigarettes, we smoked them *indoors*. Everyone said to open a window, so I did, but they hadn't meant that one— obviously—because then the air conditioner was violently sucked out and we heard it smashing against the pavement five flights below.

"Somebody could have been killed!" is what people said when I told the story, but not really; the window was above an airshaft. I was at work at the magazine the next day when my father called. I was about to tell him about the air conditioner when he said that he had cancer, that it was too far along for surgery, and that the prognosis was not good.

I met the blond boy at a party on someone's rooftop soon afterward. I felt dazed in the soggy, still night. He said that his mother had an extra air conditioner in the basement of her apartment building, and that he would help me get it downtown and up the five flights of stairs into the window I had idiotically opened. He was muscular and determined and he got it done a few days later. Then he slept over.

I had thought he would be very square because he was athletic and always clean but instead he was urgent and uninhibited and said what he wanted and knew, somehow, exactly what I wanted. He left very early the next morning before my father came over on his way to see an oncologist in Midtown.

"If only they had found it sooner," I said, pleading.

"Yeah," said my father, "and if only I had two penises I could be in the circus."

WHEN I WAS SMALL—still in my Neil Reardon phase—my father would wash my hair and call me Mrs. Rosenbaum and pretend that his name was Gladys and that we were at a beauty parlor. "We're just going to touch up your roots, Mrs. Rosenbaum," he'd say, lathering my head with baby shampoo and speaking in the accent of his own Bronx childhood. "Have you heard about Doris Kaplan? She got a bad perm in Miami. Well you know how Doris is, Mrs. Rosenbaum. With her it's always *something.*"

When I was a little older, we would take the train into the city from Larchmont and go to the Metropolitan Museum of Art. My father liked to sit out on the steps in front before we went inside, so he could watch the people emerging from the museum and see what color entry tags were in use that day. Once he knew, we'd walk up and down the steps looking for discarded tags in the correct color, and he'd be terrifically pleased if we found two to put on before we waltzed inside, past the admission booth, toward the Temple of Dendur.

In the summertime, I went to a hippie sleepaway camp in New Hampshire, where I learned songs by the Weavers and burned myself on the hot glue gun I used to make puppets out of felt and twigs. My father, Robert, sent me letters in the voice of my lisping imaginary little brother, Baby Wobbie: "I got in twubble today faw picking my nose. Mommy said I had to go to my woom but instead I hid in da cwoset and scawed da bejesus out of hew. Pwease come home soon. I miss you a wot."

CANCER. CANCER. AT WORK, at bars, at my friend's apartment on St. Marks Place, with the incompetent air conditioner the blond boy had hauled up there whirring feebly in the background, I thought, *Cancer.* Or sometimes, *My fa-*

ther is dying. It seemed surreal and made everything else seem surreal, too, because if this was possible, what else was possible?

It was oddly exhilarating—not the prospect of my father dying, but the way things could change, just like that. Had that window faced the street, I *could* have killed somebody with that air conditioner, and then that would be the truth from then on, forever. Life, so plodding and seemingly circumscribed, was labile, fragile.

And then, just like that, the prognosis changed. He would live! "Most men die *with* prostate cancer, not *of* it," my stepmother said, and now it seemed clear that my father would be among them. The doctors *would* operate; I went down to Washington for the surgery. It was terrifying to see my father afterward, all blanched and gray in the hospital bed. "Get me out of here," he said when we were alone in the recovery room. "I mean it. You're *blood.* Get me home, now."

There wasn't much to it: I told my stepmother (firmly) and the doctor (obsequiously) that my father would not be staying another night in the hospital; we were going to go home, now. But I felt fleetingly and poignantly heroic. My father had his wishes, and I would see to it that they were carried out. I was his only child. I was his dutiful son! I was *blood.*

Order was restored. The window would always face an airshaft. The grim prognosis would be a mistake. Nothing really bad could happen to me in my movie, because I was the protagonist.

5

WE MET IN THE MIDDLE OF A BLACKOUT.

It was searing hot and there wasn't any running water and New York City had lost its mind. People were sweaty and edgy, thronging the streets, leaking heat and anxiety. Traffic lights dangled dead over the intersections; taxis lurched through the dark. The ATMs didn't work and bodegas were charging insane amounts for bottled water and I was thirsty, hungover, and almost out of cash. I felt defenseless every time I walked up the ten flights to my apartment, carrying a lit candle in the ghostly stairwell.

I was nearing panic when a friend called and told me he had the water back on in his building down by City Hall, and a grill out on the balcony. As I walked there, on the cobblestone street just north of Washington Square Park, past an intersection where a woman in a sundress was directing traffic, down into the lighting district—window after window teaming with powerless, shimmering chandeliers, the people in the apartments above drinking beer on their fire escapes—the city seemed less like a nightmare and more like a carnival. My friend had said he had a house-guest in town, visiting from California: Lucy. She was golden-skinned and green-eyed in her white shirt, and she smiled with all the openness in the world when I walked in the door. She had the radiant decency of a sunflower.

It felt as if I had conjured her out of the dark. Not just the bewitched darkness of the blackout, but all the nights that had come before then, when I went to bars and parties, searching for someone who wasn't there. But she was here now.

The sky was soft and humid, up above the steaming side-walk. Our friend grilled all the meat that had thawed since his freezer had lost power and Lucy told me about the San Francisco Bay Area, where she had lived for twenty years, where I was going soon, by chance, to report a story. I was immediately struck by her wholesomeness—her clean, easy competence. I liked that she was a decade older than I was, that she was an athlete, that she had a real job, as the direc-tor of development for an environmental nonprofit, and that she owned her own home. All the girls—and the boys before them—whom I'd dated lived in rentals furnished with dusty junk. I could feel her ambition buzzing away like mine, just under her joie de vivre. I'd never thought it possible to have such a crush on someone so obviously suit-able for me in every way. My fantasies about Lucy were extravagantly domestic, almost immediately.

It would have been easy to sleep over that night. I could

have said I didn't want to go back to my hot, dark apartment. I could have stayed on the couch, and Lucy and I could have found a way to kiss, at least. But I walked home, swooning in the summer night. I didn't want an encounter. I wanted a partner.

Only she lived with another woman—Lucy was wearing a ring when we met. They had a house in Oakland, with a slate patio and leggy nasturtiums in the backyard. Lucy told me about terracing the garden in one of the first emails she wrote to me, about how she'd studied the slope and carefully planned the drainage before she planted Meyer lemons and lavender. I was dazzled: Could there really be someone so wise as to understand *drainage*?

We started writing each other incessantly. I would rush home from things to check my computer (there were no iPhones yet; I didn't even have a cell). She told me about the summer she helped build her brother's log cabin on Orcas Island: "There were only three of us living in tents on the property. We flossed, we hammered, we went swimming in the Strait of Juan de Fuca." Everything she did sounded upbeat and virtuous.

Lucy grew up in a little town in Washington State, where you could smell wood pulp from the paper mills when the wind blew. Her father, a tall, competent man who had served in MacArthur's honor guard in the Pacific theater during World War II, was the town doctor for half a century. When Lucy was little, they used to go to a cabin on the

Toutle River during the summertime, and her father lifted giant rocks and rearranged them to make her a paddling pool. He would introduce her to people by saying, "My daughter is six years old"—or "seven," or "thirteen"—"and she's never done a single thing wrong."

When she was a child, Lucy asked her parents to call her Joe—which they did, blissfully (or willfully) unaware that it was a harbinger of her homosexuality. She would borrow her brother's summer-camp uniform to survey the neighborhood, and patrol the perimeter of Lake Sacajawea wearing his coonskin cap. In the fourth grade, she came very close to convincing a new girl in school that she was a boy named Joe, and that they should go steady. Lucy got in trouble when their teacher found out about it, but she hadn't meant to be duplicitous. To her, it was the truth.

When I went to San Francisco for my story a month after the blackout, I stayed at a guesthouse near Dolores Park. Lucy picked me up in a convertible she had rented for the day, and took me to see Muir Woods. I dressed carefully for the occasion, in a pair of tiny red shorts and the hiking boots I'd bought to go trekking in the Himalayas years before. I told Lucy about that trip as we tramped through the cool shade of the redwoods, the clean smell of forest rot rising around us.

I had traveled across Asia for six months with a backpack when I was twenty-two. My mood on those exotic days in Katmandu and Da Nang alternated between euphoria and lonely terror. I had traveler's checks that I kept with my passport in a little sack that I wore under my T-shirt at all times, afraid that someone would snatch it and then I would be completely fucked. American Express let you receive mail at their offices then, and the first thing I did whenever I got to a city after a long bus ride was rush to collect a small stack of envelopes and postcards. Then I would read my mail and cry in my tea.

I had planned to stay for two weeks at a monastery in southern Thailand that hosted a silent meditation retreat for novices. The night I arrived, it was too late to go to the huts with the other foreigners; the monk who met me at the gate brought me to what had once been a stable. Lying on my sleeping bag on the straw floor, I could see the moon in the dark, shining sky out the open window. I heard animals, small and busy, moving up in the rafters. I did not feel frightened or alone.

The next morning the monk came back and took me in his truck up the road to a place where strange young white people with dreadlocks went about their chores, stone-faced. In addition to being silent, we were not supposed to read or write while we there. I lasted three days.

That trip was like all my life, distilled: a compulsion to thrust myself toward adventure, offset by a longing to crawl into the pouch of some benevolent kangaroo who would take me bounding, protected, through life. Lucy said she had gone backpacking once in Kanchenjunga. "At the end of the trek, the Sherpas told me they had given me a nickname," she said. "'Boy Scout Lady.'"

A WILD FLOCK OF green parrots had migrated to Telegraph Hill at the turn of the millennium, and I could hear them, flutelike, in the sky when we drove back to the city in Lucy's red convertible. She took me to the Zuni Café, where there was a long copper bar and the air smelled like wood smoke and rosemary, and a dazzlingly butch woman made us tequila gimlets. It was clear that I needed to move to San Francisco, immediately. Once we lived together, I figured, Lucy and I would go for drinks at that bar at least once a week—it would be one of our things.

When it started getting dark outside, she had to go. She kissed me goodbye on the corner of Gough Street and Market, and I drifted off down the hill feeling molten and golden and saved.

She came to New York often for work. I had just moved into a cacophonous apartment on Fourteenth Street— when ambulances went screeching past every fifteen minutes on their way to Beth Israel, it felt like they were plowing directly through the living room. I scheduled a housewarming party when I knew Lucy would be in town, but pretended it was an accident. The night before, she stayed up late with me making deviled eggs. Lucy told me about wandering her small town with her brothers as a child, plucking apples and plums from the neighbors' trees: "The fruit tour," she called it. With this person, I could be normal, content, blessed. Cleaned by her goodness.

A more-or-less-married forty-one-year-old who is secretly renting convertibles and flying to New York City to see her twenty-eight-year-old mistress might not sound like someone with a contagious case of virtuousness. But Lucy's relationship was over. After a very short time, it seemed more like she was cheating on me when she went home to her girlfriend than the other way around. Not that the thought of them together made me jealous or angry: It made me sad. It pained me to think of Lucy feeling lonely, out of place, in her own house.

I didn't want her girlfriend to suffer. But I didn't feel particularly guilty, either. They seemed so far from love, I even thought (stupidly) that the girlfriend might be happy to have Lucy taken off her hands.

They had become strangers. Maybe they always had been. And we were magic.

6

WE WROTE OUR VOWS IN CALIFORNIA, THE SUMMER BEFORE
I turned thirty. Lucy was getting her house ready for sale,
renovating the only bathroom with the help of a friend, so
we peed in the backyard and took showers with the garden
hose. At dusk, we sat on the deck with Paolo, her irate gray
cat, and drank vodka sodas with Meyer lemon juice—West
Coast Sparklers, we named them. "I promise to take care of
you even if you get sick or less attractive" was one vow. "I
promise not to be too controlling in the garden" was another. And our favorite: "I promise to make life a party."

And we did. On the weekends, we drove to Bolinas for
oysters, or we went swimming at the nude beach in Marin.
We went hiking and looked for eagles. We went for Mexican food in Oakland and Japanese food in Berkeley and
back to the Zuni Café, where we always ordered the roast
chicken for two. And everywhere we went, we drank: margaritas, gimlets, Prosecco, Manhattans. There was so much
to celebrate.

We shared an explosive enthusiasm that we blasted out of our bodies with alcohol. It was almost a sport. We tore through sobriety together, drink by drink, until we occupied a separate reality from the rest of the world. Late at night we'd go reeling into the Lexington, a lesbian bar in the Mission, to watch the girls with mullets and pierced noses and tattoos playing pool and hooking up, being defiant in a way that neither of us ever would. (We liked being wild, but not nearly as much as we liked being acceptable.) We had brutal hangovers, but we had them *together*. They were, in their own excruciating way, almost as much fun as the inebriation that preceded them. We would wake up bleary, still drunk, unified in our desperation for water, Alka-Seltzer, and ginger ale, laughing at our pain, at the things we'd said the night before and the people we'd encountered. We would cling to each other on the couch, while Paolo went about his business, humping the fur off of his stuffed bunny.

I had the worst hangover of my life on a road trip we took along the Oregon coast that summer, when we stayed at the motel in Cannon Beach where Lucy had gone on family vacations growing up. We went to her favorite restaurant, which looked like a log cabin, and ate lasagna and meatloaf and drank a bottle of Oregon pinot noir. For dessert we bought a flask of bourbon to drink on the balcony of our motel room. Sitting on plastic lawn chairs with the green polyester bedspread over our laps, we tried to figure out which of the dark figures in the sea were pelicans and which were just rocks. At first we had giddy but clear vision, but then we passed the bottle back and forth until the stars and the sand and the water blurred together.

In the morning the tide had come in and the waves crawled right up to the sliding glass doors of our room. I felt like I had been beaten up in my sleep and left with a head full of shrapnel. My mouth watered until I retched in the toilet, and then I lay on the bathroom floor sweating and hating myself until I was able to throw up again. I wondered why I had done this again, poisoned myself, what crime I was punishing. This continued for hours, and then Lucy went into town and came back with Tylenol and a vanilla milkshake. "Drink this," she said. "No more white devil's firewater for you." I sucked it through a straw and the sea air blew in through the sliding glass door, cleaning me, while she held me on the bed. I felt better, and then I felt blessed.

IT WAS 2004. THAT WINTER, President George W. Bush had announced his support for a constitutional amendment banning same-sex marriage in his State of the Union address. In defiance, the newly elected mayor of San Francisco, Gavin Newsom, had directed his clerks to start issuing marriage licenses to gay couples. In May, Massachusetts became the first state in America to legalize same-sex civil marriages. There were photographs in the newspaper of couples kissing on the front steps of City Hall in Boston, in San Francisco. At that particular time, it seemed like there was something more than just romantic about getting married. It seemed almost righteous.

But I was reluctant to appear greedy for arriviste credibility. I was newly (and not entirely) gay; Lucy was only my second real girlfriend. I had tried to slide casually in a dykeward direction without attracting too much attention from my skeptical friends. (In college, when I was having my first fling with another girl, Emma and I went shopping one afternoon with Matt, my closest friend from Larchmont, at a vintage clothing store. I tried on a pair of men's pants that I thought would impress my new lesbian posse, and when I looked in the mirror, I saw Matt and Emma behind me rolling their eyes.) My parents were a non-issue. "Are you impressed by how cool with this I've been?" my father had asked me when I brought my first girlfriend to his house for a weekend. I thought about it for a minute and answered, earnestly, "Not really."

Getting married to a woman seemed like an act of solidarity with a movement that I was not really entitled to be part of. "Oh give me a break!" said Lucy (a *real* lesbian with impeccable credentials and decades of experience in the field). "The whole point is that everybody gets to marry the person they love."

"I PROMISE TO TREAT your family as my family" was another vow we came up with. But it was tricky. My family was so boundary-averse, so unabashedly forward, and Lucy was so reserved. She closed in like a sea anemone when they poked at her with questions.

I didn't know how to act around her mother. She was eighty-two when we met, a Minnesotan who never said anything harsher than "Oh, honestly." It was best to talk about the garden, I learned, her towering rhododendrons and perfectly pruned roses. Or fashion: We would look at women's magazines together in the evenings while Lucy and her father watched sports on television. If it was winter, we'd flip through the thick Nordstrom holiday catalog, and her mother would say, "That's a darling heel," or, "That looks like a toasty coat." We avoided all discussion of politics, sexuality, ethnicity, and religion (except once, when I let loose an "Oy vey," and Lucy's mother said, "What?" And I said, "That's what my people say when we mean 'Oh, honestly' ").

They still lived in the house where Lucy grew up. There was still wallpaper printed with cars and trucks in the "boys' room." One of the boys was an Evangelical minister in his fifties; another had become an anesthesiologist; the youngest worked in marketing for the creationist movement. When Lucy came out in college, her parents did not speak to her for months. She had finally done a single thing wrong.

"WHAT ABOUT FIDELITY?" Lucy said that evening on the back deck, with the vows and the West Coast Sparklers, while the cool California dusk settled on the yard.

I said, "I don't think I can promise that for an entire life-time." I said, "Is that really even important?"

I sort of hoped that once you'd made a declaration of commitment to someone you truly loved you would stop feeling sodden with lust for relative strangers. But also, I sort of thought, *Who cares?* Who cares if sometimes you bring out your seduction skill set—briefly!—for a person other than your spouse and you have a little adventure with your body? Why did that have to be at your spouse's expense? Couldn't you promise your deepest love, your first allegiance, to your favorite person without locking yourself in a chastity belt and presenting her with the key?

Gay marriage wasn't even legal—we were making it up! Couldn't we invent something truer, deeper, finer than an institution devised to consolidate property and bloodlines? *We have our freedom, we can make our own rules.* Why not?

For years, I would resent that Lucy had chosen not to hear me when I told her—from the very beginning!—that I did not really value monogamy. Eventually, it would occur to me that I had chosen not to hear that it was important to *her.*

NEITHER OF OUR MOTHERS was particularly thrilled when we said we'd decided to have a wedding. Lucy's mother shuddered when we told her—it may have been the most heartfelt "Oh, *honestly*" of her life. And I could sort of see her point. She was mortified by the notion of a lesbian wedding, worried we were making a mockery of a traditional institution and therefore rejecting her values. When I asked her to help me pick the flowers for the occasion, she said tightly, "I'm sure you'll figure something out."

My own mother's contention that weddings were mainstream, commercial hoo-ha—and that marriage was no great shakes, either—seemed equally persuasive. She was as mortified as Lucy's mother by what we were suggesting, worried we were embracing a traditional institution and therefore rejecting her values. "How can you justify spending so much money on a single day?" she wanted to know. "What do you care about society's approval?" Wasn't it enough just to love each other?

It was not. I wanted more than love; I wanted marriage. Or at least that's what I thought.

OUR WEDDING, AT MY father and stepmother's house in Virginia, on the wet grass, with the sunflowers strung to the fence posts, and the last-minute decision by Lucy's parents to get up out of their seats with the help of their walkers and canes to accompany their only daughter down the aisle, was one of the great days of my life—one of the perfect, shining days. There were pink margaritas and paper lanterns floating in all the trees. There was Jesse, my oldest friend, who grew up around the corner from my house in Larchmont, playing "Crimson and Clover" on his guitar to start the ceremony. There was Emma, in a pink dress, standing behind me with Matt, but this time they weren't rolling their eyes. All of Lucy's brothers came, even the creationist. My mother wore high heels and makeup for the first time I can remember. Lucy's mother presented her with the navy handkerchief that her own mother had given to her on her wedding day in 1948.

"Something blue," she said.

I HAD WORRIED ABOUT many things in relation to marriage during the preposterously intense and consuming period of shoe shopping and ruthless guest-list pruning and tent stress leading up to that day in Virginia when we walked down the mountain in front of all of our friends and family, and decided that we were married. (Gay married, that is, fake married, because you could only really do it legally at the time in Canada, San Francisco, or Massachusetts, and what was the use of being legally married exclusively when you were in Canada, San Francisco, or Massachusetts?) I worried, for example, about being "heteronormative"—which is something I would say as a joke because it's a made-up word from the land of academic absurdity—but I didn't really care about marriage being too straight, at least not in the sense of too heterosexual. I cared about marriage being too normal, too American, too confining for my fantasy of a life.

It had not occurred to me, however, to worry about something that started happening almost immediately after our wedding: "How's your wife?" Your *wife*. People did not ask me that with a sneer. They used that word to be respectful, politically correct, and, to the best of their abilities, accurate. But it was all wrong. *I am the wife,* I wanted to tell them. *I am the girl.*

Years later, I wrote a profile of Edith Windsor, the eighty-four-year-old plaintiff in the Supreme Court case that would strike down the Defense of Marriage Act and effectively legalize same-sex marriage in America. Edie wore pearls and satin shirts and a bob she kept platinum-blond with Clairol No. 103. One night, when I was staying over at her house on Long Island and she was puttering around in a pair of leopard-print underpants, she told me of her late partner, "Every time someone calls her my wife, I am furious!" They had been together for more than forty years. "You can say she's my spouse or you can say she's my butch. But you cannot say she's my wife—it's a fucking insult!"

That was how I felt. It was not incidental to me—to either of us—that Lucy was butch. Lucy did the driving. She brought our suitcases in from the car. She raked the leaves in the fall; she got up on the roof and cleaned the gutters. She decided how we invested our retirement accounts and ultimately it was our understanding that she would be the one who made the money, who had the real responsibility for our security. I never once took out the trash unless Lucy was out of town or sick in bed.

I was our social secretary. I made our dinner plans and scheduled our dentist appointments. If there was a problem between us, it was my job to bring it up and to shepherd us to some kind of resolution. I put our pictures in photo albums and decorated our home and made my mother's chicken cutlets for dinner. "Have you ever seen Lucy in a dress?" Emma asked me once. *Don't be ridiculous!* Lucy in a dress would look like she was in drag.

I *am the wife. Lucy is my husband.*

There was never any question that if we had a child, I would bear it, and not because I was younger.

7

ONE AFTERNOON, LUCY AND I SAT ON THE LIVING ROOM floor in the house we'd bought on Shelter Island, and made a Plan. We unrolled a piece of butcher paper on the coffee table and wrote a time line of things that we wanted to have happen: SunUp, the solar panel design and installation company that Lucy had just started, would open an office in Los Angeles in 2009. I would become a foreign correspondent in 2010. We ate popcorn out of an orange enamel pot and we drew illustrations—a palm tree next to Lucy's company, a passport and a pen next to my expanded career. In the space between 2011 and 2012 I tried to draw a picture of a baby, but he came out looking like a smiling tooth. Lucy was able to fix him up, and she added a talk bubble emerging from his mouth in which she wrote, "Do I even exist?"

It was summer and we lived with all the windows and doors open; Paolo would come in and out and glare at us. With the money from the sale of Lucy's place in Oakland,

we'd bought the cottage from a Vietnam vet who loved day-
lilies; he told us how he'd tried to grow them in the front
yard. He had sprayed the flowers with the dried coyote
blood you can buy from garden centers to scare off deer,
but the smell took him back to the battlefield, corpses rot-
ting in the grass. By the time we moved in, there were no
flowers.

We put in a ton of them. My mother had taught me
about plants, about digging up the dirt and feeling the
damp, grainy earth under your fingernails. When I was
young she had showed me to make a hole big enough to
hold the root ball of a new plant with lots of good, loose soil
all around it, so the plant could stretch out without having
to fight the compacted ground. My father loved to garden,
too, especially in the damp places where moss spread and
ferns multiplied. My parents had been happy in the backyard, adding more daffodils every fall, planting more small,
hopeful trees. Whatever disappointments and cruelties they
exchanged, they were unified in their love for growing
things.

Lucy built raised beds out of cedar planks behind our
house, where we put tomatoes, tufts of catmint for Paolo,
and tulips that the deer ate before they bloomed. I dug giant
holes behind the back deck for hulking wisteria, and over
the years, the vines swallowed up the tacky railing just as I'd
hoped they would: By late May, if you looked out the
kitchen window, all you saw was a tangle of electric-green
foliage floating above the deck. We never hung curtains on

the windows in front of the house; we planted a wall of oak-leaf hydrangeas that screened the front bedroom with brown stalks and white blossoms. You could walk around that room naked in the summer under the ceiling fan and feel the whirring, wet air on your skin and nobody would see you but the sparrows.

When our house had gone up in 1918, it was three rooms, covered in shake shingles, with pine plank floors and eyebrow windows in the attic. Later, the kitchen was added on the back, along with the bedroom that became ours, from which we could see a sliver of creek from our window. There were two guest rooms in front with old crystal doorknobs, and a beat-up bathroom in between them where we glued postcards and photographs all over the walls. We put an offer on the house the day we saw it, the first time Lucy had ever set foot on Shelter Island.

She loved everything about the place: the town dump, where you had to go because there was no garbage pickup; the post office, where you got your mail because there was no delivery service. Tasks that were obsolete in the city brought you together with your neighbors on the island in a kind of benign intimacy that reminded Lucy of her childhood, and me of a book I'd loved about an extended family of bears living harmoniously in treehouses in the forest. People didn't lock their doors. A placard on the wall behind the bar at the Chequit inn read SOMEHOW, THIS STRONG SMALL ISLAND WILL SURVIVE.

Finally there was a place—for everything! Lucy's garage-

sale golf clubs. The quilt with yellow stars from my stepmother. Books that we'd read, that we hadn't yet read, that
we'd never read, all on shelves. The things that for years had
remained in our parents' homes while we went about our
young adulthoods inhabiting small spaces in big cities we
brought to that house, and they comforted us. We were
home.

During the mornings, I would write at my desk, looking
out the window at the hydrangeas, and Lucy would sit at
the kitchen counter on one of the tall orange stools, making
calls and working on her computer. As I wrote I would hear
the rattle of the cubes in her iced coffee and listen to her
talking to people on the phone: "We've had a lot of success
with that kind of application." She would explain how the
solar panels worked; how long it would take for the energy
savings to amortize the installation costs. She sounded confident and sharp. Sometimes it scared me that she'd invested her life savings in a company she'd cooked up out of
nothing. Other times it seemed like the beginning of a life
perfected.

I was thirty-two—which really seemed like the tail end
of my twenties, still. I felt as young as spring. When my
mother was that age, she had already had me, after trying
for five years. But it was different now. None of my good
friends had babies. Not Emma, my second self, who had
moved to Los Angeles to become an actress and live surrounded by otherworldly foliage in a little apartment on
Whitley Avenue. Not Matt and Jesse, my friends since

childhood; they had day jobs at websites and played in a band at bars on the Lower East Side at night. All of us still drank too much. All of us assumed we still had time for re-invention.

The dream of the dubious tooth baby could stay safely in the future. The important thing was to be married, and that I had already accomplished on my own smug, nontradi-tional terms. It was unseemly how successful I felt.

Women of my generation were given the lavish gift of our own agency by feminism—a belief that we could de-cide for ourselves how we would live, what would become of us. Writers may be particularly susceptible to this out-look, because we are accustomed to the power of author-ship. (Even if you write nonfiction, you still control how the story unfolds.) Life was complying with my story.

There were shadows I saw out of the corner of my eye that looked like problems waiting to become real, but you never know with shadows.

8

"JESUS," SAID MY FATHER, WHEN I CALLED TO TELL HIM I'd been hired to write for *The New Yorker*. "Well, nowhere to go but down."

Nobody could quite believe it. My new boss sent me a bouquet of exotic tropical flowers—birds-of-paradise and mysterious spikes—with a card that read, "Welcome to the Secret Treehouse. As ever, David Remnick." I read it out loud to Lucy, who said, "Are you sure it doesn't say, 'As if'?"

It happened fast. I met Remnick at a book party for an anthology of essays I'd contributed to about Hillary Clinton, who had not yet lost the Democratic presidential nomination to Barack Obama. But to me, *Remnick* was the president. He was the keeper of a realm so rarefied I'd barely aspired to enter it. "What's your deal?" he asked when we were introduced. "Can you write something for us?"

I understood that he meant a single article, an audition. But I would have had to quit my job at *New York* magazine to give him that, which was of course out of the question.

"Well, you could hire me," I heard myself say. "But we're not going to have a quickie."

As soon as it came out of my mouth I wanted to vanish. But Remnick smirked.

We went for lunch at a sushi restaurant near his office a few weeks later. I was so nervous I started sweating profusely, like Albert Brooks in *Broadcast News*—so much that when the waiter came by with hot towels, Remnick said, "Get those away from her!"

He asked me what I thought *The New Yorker* needed, and I said, "*The New Yorker* is perfect."

Remnick rolled his eyes.

So I told him I thought that if aliens had only *The New Yorker* to go by, they would conclude that human beings didn't care that much about sex, which they actually do. I was about to eat some seaweed when something else— something true, even—occurred to me: *I* write about sexuality and gender. I do stories about women who are *too much*. The notion of him hiring me suddenly seemed almost reasonable.

I told Remnick about a profile I wanted to write about a woman named Lamar Van Dyke. At the peak of the women's movement in the seventies, she had been the leader of a gang of lesbian separatists—a *van* gang—a pack of women who decided to live out of their VW buses, cruising the highways of North America, stopping only on "womyn's land" where men were banned. There were plenty of separatist groups with encampments at that time: the Gutter

Dykes, in Berkeley; the Gorgons, in Seattle; the Furies, in Washington, D.C.; the Radicalesbians, in New York City — along with my personal favorite, the New York Lesbian Food Conspiracy. All of them had the same basic notion: Why capitulate, why compromise, when you could separate? Live in a world of your own invention, according to whatever rules you chose.

The Van Dykes had determined that America was suffering from "testosterone poisoning," and vowed that they would speak to men only if they were waiters or mechanics. They refused to go by the last names that had been handed down to them by their husbands and fathers. Instead, they would all change their names to Van Dyke and ride forward into a glorious and liberated tomorrow. It was perfect: "Van Dyke" was accurate and tough-sounding and proclaimed to all the world, "I am a real, live lesbian." They had a dream that someday, somewhere, a maître d' would call out, "Van Dyke, party of four?" and dozens of lesbians would stand up, to the horror of the assembled heterosexuals. (Possibly the least realistic aspect of their fantasy was the notion that at any given restaurant, at any given moment, there are *dozens* of lesbians waiting for a table.)

It was the first story I worked on after I was hired. I went to Seattle and spent days listening to Lamar's stories in the crazy little house where she settled after she stopped living on the road: She had decorated it with bowling balls, a vintage barber's chair, purple crystals, and massive paintings of bright, sinister bird people. She was six feet tall with a haircut that reminded me of Johnny Cash and tattoos winding up and down both arms, many of which she had done herself. Lamar was the baddest, butchest dyke I'd ever met, a great big pirate of a woman. As she put it, "If you look at me, there's no question about it: I'm a dyke. I am gay. If you don't think so, there is something really wrong with you." But she wasn't just tough, she was *fun*, "the Merry Prankster of the women's movement," as one of her ex-husbands described her (there were three of them before she discovered lesbianism).

It was a story about the way the counterculture of the sixties and seventies promised a life of radical rebellion, and about what happened after the romance of revolution burned off. "Gay marriage and gays in the military? *That's* what you guys have come up with?" Lamar asked me at one point, incredulous, disheartened. "Your generation wants to fit in," she charged (not, I felt, unfairly). "*I want to be just like you*—that's your deal. That's the last thing I want." She shook her head. "We didn't sit around looking at our phone or looking at our computer or looking at the television. We didn't sit around looking at *screens*. We didn't wait for a screen to give us a signal to do something: We were off doing whatever we wanted."

I felt abashed, because of course I *was* gay married. I *did* want to fit in. And I didn't have any tattoos. But I was also pleased that this insurrectionist's story would be told not in a women's studies textbook or on a website about queer history, but in *The New Yorker*, where it would be read by hundreds of thousands of people all over the world who might be surprised to find it there.

IF I ADMIRED THE BADASS Van Dyke way of life, I also craved something they had categorically renounced: money. For a girl from Larchmont, I had a peculiar sense of urgency about insulating myself from a kind of privation I'd only read about in books and heard about from my blintz-making Russian grandmother, Tanya. For as long as I can remember, I have felt the shtetl nipping at my heels.

My grandmother's family fled Russia for Cuba in the hull of a ship. Tanya often talks about her childhood in Havana, running across the rooftops, the soft sounds of Spanish rising up from the street below. Her family moved again, to Chicago in 1932, and when she was nineteen she married my grandfather, Albert—Big Al—a golden-skinned Sephardic man whose parents had immigrated to America from Turkey and Greece.

Grandpa Albert saw himself as cunning, street-smart: He liked to see what he could get away with. "Heads or tails?" he'd ask his children, and then flip them for their allowance, double or nothing. Opportunity, he believed, was always lurking. Once a man he did business with in Chicago gave Al tickets to a baseball game: The man encouraged Al to borrow his good suit and his Cadillac for the occasion. Al was shot at as he drove away from the ballpark dressed in the other man's clothes, behind the wheel of the other man's car.

After he had children, Albert opened a variety store on Main Street in Racine, Wisconsin, called Premium Sales. He could never resist a truckload of ill-gotten tomatoes or a cache of transistor radios of dubious origin; Premium Sales stocked a baffling variety of merchandise as a result. There were ornamental braids of fake garlic, gold coins and jewelry, trick carnations that spewed water, placemats printed with the flags of many nations, Madame Alexander dolls, which my mother coveted as a child. Albert's mistress, Dolly, worked at the store. My mother remembers Albert taking her with him to Dolly's house on Christmas morning to deliver presents.

Like the man my mother would select years later for her own adultery, Grandpa Albert was shady, but he was charismatic, and he could be lavish: When we came to visit, if he was flush, he took us out for lobster tails and filet mignon. He had a toilet seat in his bathroom made of clear Lucite embedded with nickels, quarters, and silver dollars. Tanya was sure she had left poverty far behind when Big Al was at the peak of his Premium Sales heyday: She had silk dresses and Estée Lauder perfume; at one point, she even had a fur.

But Al was not the savvy businessman he imagined himself to be. After he filed for bankruptcy, agents came to collect their valuables for resale, and Tanya found herself hiding jewelry in her brassiere, as her mother had taught her to when they left Cuba, the posts of pearl earrings pricking at her breasts once again. She took what she could and they downsized from their ranch house in Racine to an apartment in Chicago, until eventually that, too, was out of reach.

Albert died bankrupt but content, his regrets and longings erased by Alzheimer's. Tanya has lived ever since off the largesse of the three most solvent of her five children, in a nursing home near my mother's house on Cape Cod. She is surrounded by Irish Catholic old ladies who grew up and then raised families of their own in the area, some of them never venturing outside of New England. Tanya is bored and feels isolated, despite my mother's best efforts to keep her entertained. My grandmother had hoped to grow old in Chicago, in a like-minded community of Jewish immigrants from Russia, Poland, and Romania—speakers of Yiddish with whom she could go to the theater or kibitz on the bus to Marshall Field. Instead, she has returned to the sense of scarcity she knew as a child. In her ninety-fourth year of life, Tanya still talks about her late husband with rancid disgust.

"Look at Grandma," my mother would say. "You never want to be dependent on a man." The fear of ending up like Tanya, cutting coupons in a one-room efficiency surrounded by strangers, made me vigilant like my parents, anxious that the poverty of our ancestors was always just one wrong move away.

LUCY WANTED TO BE WEALTHY, too. She grew up as I did, with her own bedroom, in a house with a garden and a green lawn, but with a sense that ruin was at a safe distance. Now she wanted to regain the privileges of her childhood, to play golf at a country club and go skiing with her brothers in the wintertime. "But mostly I just want the experience of success again," she told me. "I want to feel how I felt as an athlete." She was the star of her high school basketball team. They had won the state championship, and Lucy was recruited to play for an Ivy League university. When she was cut from the team during her freshman year, it had devastated her. She had tears in her eyes when she told me about it.

She wanted to redeem herself with her business. "Imagine if there were solar panels on all the rooftops of Manhattan," she said, "then Los Angeles, and eventually every city in the country." The world would be a slightly better place, she'd sell her business, and we'd be rich.

Clearly, it was necessary for me and Lucy to transition out of a drunken youth of whiskey shots at three in the morning into a sophisticated adulthood of a little wine with dinner. We had to do this to progress along our time line, I argued, in order to hit our marks. She would never be able to dominate the world of green business with a hangover. I had a job at *The New Yorker* now, for crying out loud— nowhere to go but down.

But that wasn't even the main thing. *What if I want a child?* For this to be an option, we had to stop getting hammered.

I was full of strategies: Let's drink only on weekends. Let's have a two-drink maximum. Let's never drink at home. Let's only drink at home. Let's never drink hard li-

quor. It irritated me that Lucy seemed less committed—
uncommitted, in fact—to my project. It irritated her that I
was making rules, and changing them, and not always following them myself.

MY SECOND ASSIGNMENT FOR *The New Yorker* was in Paris.
I had been there once before, and all of my research and
preparation had proved worthless on that trip: I'd arrived at
Charles de Gaulle and immediately gotten on the wrong
bus, ended up on the wrong side of the Seine, and gotten in
a taxi that took me to the wrong hotel and cost all of my
cash. Then I'd burst into tears on a park bench just before a
French pigeon shat on my head. So I was disproportionately
pleased when Lucy's old friend DJ told me a few days before
I left for my story that he had the time and the frequent-flier
miles to accompany me to France—he had just broken up
with his boyfriend and he was dying for distraction.

This time, the weather was luminous. The map made
sense. We stayed in a tiny room in the elegant Hôtel Montalembert in Saint-Germain-des-Prés, where the magazine
had put me up. There was a bottle of Champagne on ice by
the bed when we arrived—I insisted that it was complimen-
tary, but DJ wouldn't let us drink it. "Don't touch that," he
told me. "It's one of their Vichy tricks."

We loved being mistaken for a married couple by the
hotel staff. "Be a good wife," DJ would say at breakfast, "and
fetch me another *saucisson*." Whenever I wasn't reporting,

DJ and I walked the streets and sat in the parks, talking about art and sex and the differences between men and women, the gay and the straight, the coupled and the promiscuous.

ME

> I think you're idealizing being in a relationship. It's not going to solve all your problems.

DJ

> Do I have a lot of problems?

ME

> Oh, please. But so do Lucy and I. They're just different problems. John Updike wrote that marriage is like two people locked up with one lesson to read, over and over, until the words become madness.

DJ

> I think my penis just fell off.

ME

> No, it's fine. I don't have to tell you how great Lucy is. We're just in a hell of our own making half the time.

DJ

> So that's marriage.

ME

If you're lucky.

We looked up his friend Sacha, who made us dinner in his bleak, modern apartment near Montmartre, which delighted us to no end because it meant we were seeing the *real* Paris. And I liked how unabashedly Sacha flirted with me. It made me feel pretty and potent.

SACHA

My girlfriend is driving me crazy. You don't understand how it is between men and women, DJ.

DJ

Whatever, Sacha. I'm completely alone in the world except for my fake wife here.

SACHA

I wish she were my fake wife.

ME

I'm already Lucy's fake wife.

One afternoon, DJ and I went to see the National Museum of Natural History because Sacha said there was amazing taxidermy there. Hordes of chic, shrieking French children ran around the stuffed elephants and bobcats, the

Noah's Ark–like procession of all creatures great and small
and stuffed.

> DJ
>
> Sometimes I watch children laughing and
> playing and think: I'm so glad I don't have
> any.

> ME
>
> It would be inconvenient right now.

> DJ
>
> I don't understand why people do it to
> themselves! I feel sorry for people with
> kids.

> ME
>
> I don't know—I think it would be cool.
> To have another person in your family who
> just came out of nowhere? Who you *made*?

> DJ
>
> It's not a gingerbread man. It changes your
> entire life.

> ME
>
> I don't know if that's a bad thing. *This* [mo-
> tioning to myself] can't be all there is.

DJ

> Well *this* [motioning to himself] can. I'm very
> disappointed in you.

WHAT I DID WITH the things Lamar Van Dyke told me in Seattle was write a story—make a meaning, impose a narrative on the information I'd gathered. That's what I do. That's what I'm doing right now. (That's also what DJ and I did when we got back from Paris: We wrote a screenplay about our trip that we were briefly convinced was going to make us rich and famous, or, at the very least, would be made into a TV movie for a gay cable channel. None of that happened.) In the narrative in my head, that trip with the Champagne in the melted ice at the Hôtel Montalembert happened when my life still fit and my marriage was imperforate. Whether that is *the* truth or merely *my* truth, whether everything would be different if I could only go back to that hotel room and warn my younger self, I'll never know.

9

ONE DAY YOU ARE VERY YOUNG AND THEN SUDDENLY you are thirty-five and it is Time. You have to reproduce, or else. By that point, many of my friends had already been working on their reproductive ambitions for quite a while.

Elisa tried for six miserable years—going to the doctor's office every morning before work to have her blood tested and her uterine lining measured. She was distraught pretty much all the time and talked of little else. Nature *owed* her this: She wanted to be a mother, which was her most basic right as a woman who'd bled once a month for twenty years. When she finally found out that she was pregnant, she ran to her boyfriend's office and pulled him out of a meeting, and they jumped up and down in a frenzy of elation and relief. A month later, she fainted on the doctor's table when he told her it was ectopic.

Erika used up all of her savings on IVF. Every other month, another twenty thousand dollars was swallowed up. We would go for long walks up the Hudson and she would cry bitterly, enraged with herself for waiting so long, furious at her body for denying her the child she was desperate to produce. Her twenties and early thirties suddenly seemed to have been utterly squandered on whatever it was she'd been doing instead of getting pregnant.

Samantha went the craziest of all of them while she was getting shot up with hormones. She was always on the brink of hysteria and entirely obsessed with having a baby—something she had been ambivalent about just months before. She hated the needles. She hated sitting in waiting rooms full of discouraged women who were hemorrhaging time and money, wondering with increasing panic after every failed attempt, *Did I miss my chance?*

For all of them, it seemed that nothing else mattered now. Only motherhood was meaningful.

OUR REPRODUCTIVE POWERS WERE first made known to us when we were early adolescents, pubescent children, really. We waited for our periods with excitement! I used to trade maxi pads with my friend Mitsu Yashiro as if they were stickers—our mothers had bought us small boxes of sanitary napkins so that we'd be ready when the big day came. We were delighted by the different silky weaves, the various crotch-conforming shapes, and the promise they held: The future is coming. That was even more exciting than the related frisson of our burgeoning sexuality. (But then, strangely, suddenly, there it was: the power to attract erotic attention, a particular kind of admiration. A kind that made you feel feminine—ladylike, even. Too loud, too assertive, too much, *too male*, is really what I had been told I was for years by teachers, other kids, my extended family. But with the arrival of this new power, I was all woman.)

After the initial thrill of the many kinds of panty liners, the sprouting breasts and blossoming hips, we were faced with the Sisyphean task of managing our fertility. Pregnancy—we were taught, if we were privileged—was something awful that went with sex, just as AIDS and genital warts went with sex, unless you used condoms (and even then, be really careful). It was made clear that sexually transmitted diseases and teen pregnancy were simply not for us: We were to use birth control and go to college and if we somehow got pregnant too soon or with the wrong guy, we were to abort. There was no mention of the possibility that we might want to get pregnant too *late*.

From the minute the dragon of our fertility came on the scene, we learned to chain it up and forget about it. Fertility meant nothing to us in our twenties; it was something to be secured in the dungeon and left there to molder. In our early thirties, we remembered it existed and wondered if we should check on it, and then—abruptly, horrifyingly—it became urgent: Somebody find that dragon! It was time to rouse it, get it ready for action. But the beast had not grown stronger during the decades of hibernation. By the time we tried to wake it, the dragon was weakened, wizened. Old.

With modern science it could be resurrected, though,

made fire-breathing once more! We would go to the clinics and the hospitals; we would flood the offices and the coffers of the reproductive endocrinologists and the obstetrician/ gynecologists and soon we'd look up and see a sky full of flying forty-year-old dragons. (Then we'd look down and see sidewalks crowded with double strollers full of twins.) The shots and the pills, the sonograms and the ultrasounds, the ICSI and ovulation induction, the treatments at the very edge of modern technology, were miserable in a way that seemed, ironically, medieval. But they were not without a whiff of excitement. Because we were playing with a power much greater than even sexuality: nature herself.

WHILE MY FRIENDS WERE becoming outraged by their inability to have children, I was tormented by a different kind of primal acquisitiveness. I was racked with lust—afflicted with and addicted to it. The entire world had shrunk down to a single point for me, the way your field of vision closes in when you're getting a migraine. And the point was sex.

When I slipped back into contact with my old lover on the morning of the lions in South Africa, I found out that she had changed. "If you saw me you might not recognize me," she wrote. She had "transitioned" into a he. I was stunned.

When we dated, Jen had never once said that she didn't feel female—I had dismissed her initially as insufficiently butch. (And then I had been shocked to find that even though she looked nothing like anyone I'd ever been attracted to before, there was a chemical current between us that kept pulling me back, whether I approved of her or not.) Who would she be as a man? What did that even mean? I had to see.

The transformation was astonishing. Instead of the girl with a catlike face and heaving gait I remembered, she — he — was a fit young man with a handsome angularity to his visage and muscular shoulders. He had stubble on his cheeks. His voice was deep and confident, nothing like the sound that had come out of her mouth when her name was Jen. It was Jim now. But I kept getting it wrong: calling the manifestly male person sitting across from me on a park bench in Greenwich Village by the name of a girl I'd known years before. And had stopped seeing because she freaked me out.

Whatever I had given Jen of myself was always insufficient. If we were spending time together and I said I had to leave, she would invariably say she was heading in the same direction and want to walk me wherever I was going. She would sometimes call and say she was in my neighborhood, and if I told her I was working, busy, whatever, she would ask if she could come up just to use the bathroom, get a glass of water — something that would make me cruel and unreasonable if I refused. Whenever possible, I had gone to her little apartment instead of inviting her to mine, because that way I could leave: If she was at my place, I would feel panic creeping up when I wanted her to go, because I knew that it would entail a protracted negotiation, probably a fight.

These examples sound benign. But everything with Jen had an unsettling undercurrent, because her fundamental drive was to push until she felt resistance, and then blast past it. She *liked* invading, intruding, conquering: finding what a person didn't want to relinquish and then taking it anyway. She didn't so much want to walk with me or come upstairs with me as she wanted to control me.

When the lights were off, that was not a problem. It was as if Jen had access to a user's manual for my body and brain that nobody else had known existed. I found her objectionable by all normal standards, but the way we connected wasn't normal: It was uncanny, extreme, unnerving. "I like that dress," she said once, about a blue terry-cloth beach cover-up I used to wear around the East Village as if it were real clothing. "I bought it for you," I told her. When I'd tried it on at the store on East Seventh Street, I knew the second I looked in the mirror that I was seeing the version of me that she craved. I wore it constantly.

Here, now, sitting in front of me, wearing jeans and a flannel shirt, drinking coffee from a paper cup, was that person—but without breasts, without the defining edge of desperation. I had met him at the worst time in his life, he said. He (she?) had been unmoored, new in New York City and bewildered by who to be. I had been something to grip, much too tightly, he admitted.

The hydrangeas around us in the Jefferson Market Garden were just letting go of their summer color. Jim seemed calm and self-assured and self-contained, an improvement on his former self in every way. He was like an ungainly shrub that had died down over the winter and come back in the spring, beautiful.

When I got home, I wondered if whatever had happened surgically, hormonally (I didn't ask for the details), had cured him of his craziness. If *I* had been born in a form that didn't fit, wouldn't it have made me feel—and seem—nuts? Sex used to transform what I couldn't stand about Jen into what I desired about her. Maybe a change of sex had likewise made any number of Jen's deficiencies into Jim's strengths, the way it had changed her shoulders from a blocky woman's into a strapping young man's.

I didn't tell Lucy about Jim. I didn't tell her because even though I decided I wouldn't see him again (and then decided, after he emailed several times, that I would have dinner with him just once), I knew at some level from the moment we got back in touch that I was about to do something terrible.

THE DIFFERENCE BETWEEN LUCY'S affair with me, and my affair with someone I was sure I'd never love, is that Lucy thought I was a ladder to a new life. I thought I was having a smutty daydream. It is Lucy's vision that sounds like fantasy—like midlife crisis, when you consider that she was in her forties, and I was in my twenties, and that we fell in love the first night we met. But it was my vision of infidelity that turned out to be delusional.

I thought I could be like a French man with a mistress in a movie . . . that I could step outside of my life for a few gleaming hours from time to time and then return to it, without consequence, or with the sole consequence being my own satisfaction (or reduced dissatisfaction). I would rush to the subway at West Fourth Street, crafting lies about where I was going the whole way there in case I ran into someone I knew. I'd take the thrilling ride across the Manhattan Bridge on the B train and look out the window at the Statue of Liberty, feeling gorgeous, treacherous, lascivious, doomed.

My mother had it all wrong: to bring that into your home, where it lies on a pile of blankets in the TV room, scaring everyone, polluting everything? Misguided. Unthinkable. But I understood, now, her dilemma. I wanted what she had wanted, what we all want: everything. We want a mate who feels like family and a lover who is exotic, surprising. We want to be youthful adventurers and middle-aged mothers. We want intimacy and autonomy, safety and stimulation, reassurance and novelty, coziness and thrills. But we can't have it all.

At first, Lucy did not notice. She was preoccupied with her company. She was anxious about it all the time and reluctant to commit to any plan that would take her away from her vigil at the computer screen, where she sat vibrating with anxiety at all hours. When she wasn't working or worrying about work, she would drink until she knocked herself unconscious, into the mercy of sleep.

But what about *me*? Me me me me me?

Virginia Woolf wrote that "showing off, which is not copulating, necessarily, nor altogether being in love, is one of the great delights, one of the chief necessities of life. Only then does all effort cease; one ceases to be honest, one ceases to be clever. One fizzes up into some absurd delightful effervescence of soda water or champagne through which one sees the world tinged with all the colours of the rainbow." My mother glowing in the clinking Mexican glasses full of 7UP. Me in my red shorts in San Francisco — someone's young and treasured girlfriend, not someone's neglected, thickening wife.

Ego. The sparkle of one's own ego pumped full of bubbles by another person's ardor, ardor that a spouse of many years can seldom muster, or maybe just doesn't bother with.

Ego, sure, but also sex. Sex that takes you — somehow! — through a portal to another world. Not just this world, in which you are this self, only lickerish: a new world, where a new self, who has nothing (but everything) to do with who you really are, comes forth. A world with its own dream logic in which the strangest things are desperately erotic — there is no predicting or explaining this; reason, like language itself, has no purchase here. Gender, too, is meaningless. Not meaningless in the tortured academic sense of being "deconstructable." Here, gender is simply beside the point. (People sometimes tell me that they're baffled by bisexuality: They are convinced that having sex with women is totally different from having sex with men. But it isn't. No more than having sex with *anyone* is totally different from having sex with anyone else.)

Reason, language, gender—and also loyalty, morality, decency—simply aren't currency in the carnal world. This world is value-neutral. This world is inside out.

Sex that accomplishes this kind of transfiguration is a drug. It is not an easy thing to deny yourself once you know exactly where to get it. When I went to that apartment high in the sky above Brooklyn, the light was always platinum and everything looked lit from within. It was as if I'd stumbled through the door that separates regular life from what could be.

Anything was possible: A woman could become a man—a rich man, at that, though it didn't make a lot of sense to me. Jim had no real job or career, but he lived in a dazzling apartment with three bedrooms and a view of the Brooklyn Bridge and the Statue of Liberty. (When we'd been involved years before, Jen had lived in a crummy apartment, like I did. We had both worked long hours, tied to our desks, and had to be careful how we spent our paychecks. His explanation for this change in fortune was that he had invested well. I suspected he'd gotten access to his family's money—which I resented and disdained. What I liked very much, though, was having someone else pick up the check.) I could be married but have a whole second life, in a different borough, with another person, whom I had very little in common with besides desire.

Every time, it was transcendent. But then I started not wanting to leave after I put my clothes on. And then I was destroyed.

LUCY WOULD BRING ME a cup of coffee in bed in the morning and I would feel the searing truth of how lucky I was to live with this person, to have this ally in life.

But I couldn't stop thinking about someone else.

It was unsolvable, unhinging. I was writing and reading about women's boxing at the time, and I was struck by Joyce Carol Oates's description of two fighters clutching each other in the ring: They form "a knot of sorts, tightly, cruelly knotted, there to be untied. You can't, but you must, untie it. You must—but you can't." I had made myself into that knot. *I love my spouse; I will not leave her. I am fixated on another person, whose attention I cannot breathe without.*

What is *happening?* Lucy asked me.

Nothing, I told her.

I feel like I'm going crazy, she said.

Maybe you're crazy but maybe you're right. It was too much: I couldn't do it. I could cheat on her—man, could I cheat—and I could betray her trust. But I could not tell her that her perceptions were wrong, that the situation around her was other than what she sensed it to be. I couldn't deprive her of her belief in her own interpretive powers. *You aren't crazy. You're right.*

I told her that I had cheated. I did not mention that I had also lost my mind.

I could prevent myself from going to Brooklyn to fornicate, but my thoughts would not stay away from that other, ungovernable world and the person who could take me there—a person whom I found baffling, disturbing, and frequently mortifying. *As if you could ever have a* child *together?* I would think, outraged by my own mutinous yearning.

Jim had said we could—should. A biological child, of sorts: He suggested I carry a baby crafted from his eggs, fertilized by donor sperm. *His* eggs. The phrase canceled itself out. And the idea infuriated me: Imagine the birth defects risked by a baby conceived from an egg that had spent years bathed in exogenous testosterone! But it wasn't just that danger or the complexity of the procedures involved that made his suggestion repellent to me. It was his sense of entitlement—his belief that you could just keep choosing whatever you wanted in life, without ever sacrificing a single thing. (And me? What did I believe? That I could be gay *and* straight? That I could be married and unhindered? A wanderer and a mother?) I wanted to believe I was different from him. (Better.) And I did not want to raise a child with someone who didn't work for a living and saw every parameter as circumnavigable.

"I *am* working," Jim told me angrily. He was writing a book about his transition. But I didn't take it seriously. In fact, like almost everything else he did, it made me irate. What I had spent fifteen years learning how to do, he had decided he could do professionally, just like that. (This had happened before: There was a time when he was going to be a singer, then an actor. But a writer? That was just offensive.)

And yet. I was unrelentingly distracted. I thought most often about the physical acts themselves, but there were corollary sensory flashes. Like: the taste of the soup at the Japanese restaurant where we went once afterward. Or: the sound of the wind in that bedroom.

I began to feel claustrophobic in my own house. I shared our cat's fevered desperation to find an open window, a door left ajar, a precious opportunity to escape and go . . . where? *I am afraid that I will pull this house apart,* I wrote in my journal. *And then it will be winter and I'll be outside, freezing.*

The thought of leaving Lucy made me feel physically ill. To abandon my best friend in the world? Unbearable. But then I was already gone. The parallel narrative of my secret, imagined other life was always swallowing my attention, the life in which I was single, vibrant, liberated.

It was awful having someone you loved swallowed up all the time. It was bad banging on the door for your mother while she dipped into her other life in the next room. But I knew now that it had been awful for her, too—that lurching between lives is hell. Even if one life is manifest and the other is mostly hypothetical, the inability to occupy your own reality is torment, is torture. It is sin and punishment all in one.

10

IF I TOOK A LONG ENOUGH FLIGHT TO A STRANGE ENOUGH place, maybe I could leave this fever dream behind. I accepted an assignment to write about the conservative politician Mike Huckabee; it was not my usual beat, but I wanted to be as far away as I could get. In January 2010, I met Huckabee in Jerusalem at the Wailing Wall. He was leading a tour group of 160 Evangelicals through the Holy Land with the singer Pat Boone. It was easy to spot them amid the black hats, the bearded men davening in front of the white-gold Jerusalem stone. Huckabee was wearing a pink shirt with white polka dots and a yarmulke. "I think what I should do is convert," he said, squinting in the sunshine. "This covers my bald spot completely."

He had a folksy self-assurance I found seductive at that fraught moment. "Character is who you are when nobody else is watching," he wrote in one of his books—the undeniable, hokey truth. (I *had* to stop cheating. I had to locate some integrity.) I was writing about Huckabee's prospects for the presidency, but what really interested me was how someone whose positions I found so upsetting could seem so decent when you spoke to him, so thoughtful, really. While the Christians were shopping for olive-wood Jesus figurines in a souvenir shop, we had a cup of tea in the back room and he told me about how he "grew up in a culture where everybody went to church but nobody took it that seriously," in Hope, Arkansas. He found the reflexive piety in his community "very pharisaical in nature" when he was young: "People would say boys and girls shouldn't go to R-rated movies, or they shouldn't swim together," he said. "I was the guy that always asked why." In high school, he was sent to the principal's office for leading a group of students in protest against the Vietnam War. "I always questioned, even when it was inappropriate to question," he told me.

But, like all of us, I guess, Huckabee questioned only the rules that struck him as questionable. He was sure, for example, that homosexuality was "unnatural and sinful," and, as governor of Arkansas, he had successfully championed laws that prevented gay people from becoming foster parents, and banned gay adoptions. "We can get into the ick factor," he told me, "but the fact is two men in a relationship, two women in a relationship, biologically that doesn't work." It didn't seem to occur to him that I might not find gayness icky. It didn't matter to him that a twenty-five-year study had just come out from the American Academy of Pediatrics concluding that children brought up by lesbian parents were better adjusted than their peers. The wrongness of gayness was something Huckabee *believed*. It was as real to him as Jim's belief that he was a man.

Huckabee's wife, Janet, was with him in Israel. They had known each other since the seventh grade. On their first date, Huckabee took her to a truck stop after he covered one of her high school basketball games for the local radio station, where he worked as a student reporter. "We started dating at seventeen, got married at eighteen," she said. "What were we thinking?"

"We weren't thinking!" Huckabee replied. "We weren't thinking at all!" I asked him what he'd learned about love as a person who'd been married for thirty-six years. "I think we both went into it understanding it was for life," he told me. "I've always said, if you believe divorce is an option, you'll take it."

AT DINNER AT THE David Citadel Hotel, I sat next to Mary, a perky woman with white hair and cornflower-blue eyes. She was very excited that I was Jewish. "I mean, you're the chosen people!" she said. Many of the Christians on the trip were passionate Zionists, at least in part because they believed that Jewish control of the territory between the River Jordan and the Mediterranean is a biblically ordained precondition for the Second Coming of Christ. (Some of them politely admitted that they had no doubt that most Israelis would be spending eternity in Hell. "That is an issue," a man named Randy told me apologetically.) But

Mary seemed ingenuously curious. She asked about how we celebrated holidays, and I told her about the Orthodox nursery school I'd attended, where I played Queen Esther in our Purim pageant, and we all ate hamantaschen and shrieked when the teacher said Haman's name. (I did not mention that my parents moved me to public school before first grade because they thought I was getting too Jewish.)

Mary told me that God spoke to her. "Don't laugh," she said, "but it's like seeing words pop up in my head the way you do on a computer screen." Her husband, who was seated to her left, was a loud, avuncular Southern man with white hair and a barrel chest—I could hear him denigrating Obama at the top of his lungs, which seemed to make Mary only slightly less uncomfortable than it made me. A few weeks before the trip, she said, when she was in the shower, seething about something he'd done, the words *I chose him for you* came up on the holy computer screen in her mind.

What peace it must be to know that someone is yours, no matter what—it is ordained, can never be otherwise. (*Motherhood*, I heard in my head.) How relaxing—how enviable—to believe that an omnipotent other has a plan for your life. Mary said she would pray to God to talk to me, too.

I thought: *I will never have that.* I had Lucy—who understandably sort of hated me and got weird and drunk on a regular basis because I was a terrible fake wife—and I had my garden and my friends and my job.

But it's more than a job, I told myself. *It's a calling!*

Seriously? was my next thought. *Writing magazine articles is your sacred duty?*

Then: *There's something of value in trying to put the world into words.*

And finally: *You spend your entire life picking people apart. You use them and then you rid yourself of them the way you want to rid yourself of your spouse.*

"You just throw away another human being like a toy you're sick of playing with?" Huckabee said the next morning. He was waiting to do a radio appearance, eating a chocolate croissant in the lobby outside the recording studio, and explaining why he did not believe in comprehensive sexual education for high school students. Information about how to prevent unwanted pregnancy would only encourage teenagers to sexually exploit and then discard each other, he reasoned, when they ought to be encouraged to save intimacy for marriage. I thought his conclusions about education were daft. But his description of a selfish beast who cares only for her own esurient desires haunted me. *You just throw away another human being?*

Who would do that?

Such a person was unworthy of love, of kin. Such a person was unfit to be a mother.

WHEN I RETURNED FROM JERUSALEM, I told Lucy that I had been heartless and selfish and greedy like a child: that

I'd had an affair because I didn't know the first thing about love. She punished me by routinely getting inebriated at the worst possible times, which I hated but knew I deserved. (It did not cross my mind that this might not be all about me.)

You have an affair because you are not getting what you want from your loved one. You want more: more love, more sex, more attention, more fun. You want someone to look at you with lust—after years of laundry—transforming you into something radiant. You want it, you need it, you *owe* it to yourself to get it. To live any other way is to be muffled and gray and marching meaninglessly toward death. You want what she gave you at the start (but what you had hoped would expand and intensify instead of shrinking until you find yourself so sad, so resentful, you can barely stand to be you).

You have an affair to get for yourself what you wish would come from the person you love the most. And then you have broken her heart and she can never give you any of it ever again.

11

WE SEPARATED FOR A WHILE. LUCY STAYED OUT ON SHELTER
Island and I found an apartment in the city. Sometimes it
was a relief to be on my own, not feeling (as) awful about
myself, not fixated on how much she'd been drinking or
what I could do to stop it. Sometimes I inhabited my life: I
looked at the trees outside my window and felt unconfused.
Other times I missed Lucy so much it was nauseating.

But I started up my affair again. *I'm separated! Why not?*
If I was going to suffer like this, there might as well be some
kind of payoff. I would get to the bottom of it. I would get it
out of my system! Addictions that are fed get worse, though,
not better.

My email account kept getting hacked. Jim denied
doing it and said it wounded him that I would accuse him
of such a thing. I told myself it was the work of a stranger,
that these things happened in the modern world. I started
feeling wary of him, though—cornered—as I had years before, when he would show up at my door without warning.

One afternoon Jim drove me to Ikea in his black car to look for a sink. I was almost weak with gratitude as we walked through the aisles of white ceramic basins with their Viking names: Odensvik; Bråviken; Hagaviken. How kind he was to bring me here, to do an errand like this with me, when I had been relegating him to the periphery of my life for as long as we'd known each other. He was guilty only of wanting to help me set up a new home, where he'd be welcome.

We got lost in the bunk-bed region on the way to the cash registers. As we wandered through the airless maze of simulated children's rooms with no exit in sight, I started to sweat. There were sheets printed with kangaroos. There were beanbags and small desks. There were blunt miniature forks and knives, and everything else you need to buy for a normal life. By the time we found an escalator going down and I paid for my Tornviken, I felt dizzy.

Back at my apartment building, Jim carried the sink up the stairs with me and asked if I wanted help installing it. I said that I would tackle it another day. "I really don't feel well," I told him when he asked to stay, which was the truth.

"Did you promise Lucy you would never let me sleep here?" he asked.

"No," I said, which was a lie.

ONE MORNING, AS I was staring at my computer, I saw something impossible. An email that Jim had written me—

in which he made his case for our relationship by recapping every detail of our affair—had been forwarded to Lucy. From my account.

Was I actually insane? Had I sent that email to Lucy in some kind of trance? Was this my monstrous way of ending our marriage?

"No, you fool," Emma said when I called. "Jim did this."

"I don't think so," I told her, and started crying. "I feel like I'm in a pressure cooker."

"Well it's turning your mind into short ribs," she said. "*Jim did this*. It couldn't be clearer."

I knew it was Jim—an incubus, it seemed, who couldn't be kept out of my mind or my home or my correspondence—but I could not quite *believe* it: "He wouldn't do anything to hurt me."

"He's a sociopath," Emma said. "And you're scaring me."

Matt told me, "You should never, ever talk to him again, for the rest of your life."

"I'm trying," I said. "It's hard."

Matt sighed. "I was watching that show *Intervention* the other night and the people sound like you: like they're missing a piece of their brains."

You have to be that way when you're addicted to something. In order to finish your cigarette, you have to cordon off the knowledge that it's killing you. (And if you are addicted, you *will*—it won't even feel like a choice.) It was not until Jim slipped and quoted something I'd written in an email to someone else, which he never would have seen if he hadn't been hacking my account, that I was forced to admit he was a liar. That he was just as crazy as a man as he'd been as a woman.

I was crazy, too, though. I had let this happen—made it happen. Extricating myself from my affair was like shattering a great pane of glass in the middle of a room: months after I'd finished cleaning up the crash, there were still shards lurking in the corners. I was still picking small, vicious slivers out of the soles of my feet.

IF YOU ARE LUCY, meanwhile, you are trying to start a company. It's a bold act, in your mid-forties, when you already have a solid career that you could continue with for another couple of decades, and then slide into a modest retirement. But you want something more: You don't want to be a cog; you want to make a new machine. You want your parents to be impressed and your wife to stop worrying.

She doesn't. In fact, when you invest—little by little— all the money you've ever made into the company, the only person who worries more than you do is your wife. *Your wife.* You changed your entire life for her. You left your girlfriend; you sold your house; you moved across the country. And it was worth it, because what you gained was the deepest adoration you'd known since childhood, when you would come home from the fruit tour to find you were the apple of your parents' eyes. That has stopped, and now the woman who worshipped you is angry at you all the time, for not having a paycheck. For drinking.

But you don't have a paycheck because you are trying to make it big—to become again the champion whom everybody cheers. (That is the side of you she fell in love with, you fear, the side she's counting on to rescue her from the sucking pull of the shtetl, where women get old before their time, eating mud-colored gruel with mouths missing half their teeth.) And what is the one thing that gives you some peace from the churning anxiety that is waking you up at two in the morning and tormenting you until the alarm goes off and it is time, again, to rise exhausted from your bed and face another day of convincing your staff and your wife and yourself that you've got it all under control? A drink. An innocent beer, like you pounded with your teammates. A vodka soda that passes as 7UP if nobody sits near enough to you to smell it at lunch. A kind, loving drink that washes away your stress and suffering as it slides coolly down your throat. Sometimes your wife says that alcohol is your mistress, that you love it more than you love her. And sometimes she's right.

Then a vile, unbearable email, written by her hideous lover—her bearded girlfriend—arrives in your in-box, announcing disgusting things, like: They have been shopping for sinks. They went to Fire Island one afternoon and walked on the beach. They have sex, lots of it. *They are in love.*

You rush out of a meeting when you read the email on

your BlackBerry, and you think you will throw up, but then you don't. Because you *know* something: They are not in love. Your wife is possessed. Her *real* self loves only you. You will remind her of this, and the nightmare will end. Your company and your marriage and *you* will succeed, if it kills you. And it may.

12

stop drinking. No more agony. No more disloyalty. We would grow up now, for real.

We moved back in with each other. On my thirty-sixth birthday, Lucy gave me an old green bicycle and a pink helmet. I started riding that green bike everywhere, thrilled to be zipping past the taxis locked in traffic and the slow-moving pedestrians clogging the sidewalks. I was fast and unfettered, flying along the Hudson, safe under my pink hard hat. Despite everything I put her through, Lucy had given me that.

One night, she called from the apartment when I was about to bike home from a party for someone at work. She was frantic: "Paolo is *dead.*" He had started making a horrible sound and then crawled under the couch. Lucy had lifted it off of him in a burst of maternal strength and then held him in her arms until his body went limp. When I got back to the apartment, Lucy was lying on the bathroom floor, sobbing next to his corpse.

Something had to be *done*—it was urgent; that much was clear. We decided that we needed to bury him, immediately, on Shelter Island. So we wrapped Paolo in a Mexican serape with his toy bunny, got in the Jeep, and started hurtling east, through the Midtown Tunnel, past the endless cemeteries of Queens, past the Paris hotel with its tree-size replica of the Eiffel Tower on top. Lucy was driving and crying and briefly convinced that Jim had broken into the apartment and poisoned Paolo. "That cat was my family," she said. That, and, "I can understand why couples break up after they lose a child."

We were well into Queens before we realized that we would never make it out in time to catch the last ferry to Shelter Island. We turned around, drove back to the apartment, and left Paolo in the cold car. Then we set out again the next morning, through the Midtown Tunnel, past the endless cemeteries of Queens, past the Paris hotel, and on toward the vineyards of the North Fork, the mariners' shops in Greenport that sell ship cleats and heavy rope. We buried Paolo with his sex bunny at the foot of a tree in the backyard, where they lie wrapped in an endless embrace in their Mexican serape.

For weeks, Lucy looked like she was about to sob. Our home felt empty without that cat; we were palpably down a man. It was a wet, gray winter and it passed slowly with very little daylight.

PERIODICALLY, LUCY WOULD STILL seem drunk.

I heard her entering the house while I was taking a

shower one afternoon, and I came out wrapped in a yellow towel, excited to see her. But I took one look and saw that it wasn't really her. There was a blurriness in her eyes, a vacated twist to her facial expression. I felt the floor turn to water under my feet. Lucy had vanished, and in her place someone furtive and messy was telling me things that didn't add up.

Sometimes her speech would be slurred, but usually it was subtle. Something would just be . . . off. Then a terrible queasiness would slither through me and come out of my mouth in different ways. Sometimes fearful, sad, pleading: "Honey, have you been drinking?" Sometimes unhinged, abject: "I can't take this anymore." Sometimes icy, condemning, ruthless: "You're the worst," I said once, and meant it. (To my best friend in the world. To the person I had slept next to on a thousand naked nights, I said, *You're the worst.*)

I would bring it up later, when she seemed normal again, present. "It's like you turn into a different person," I'd say. I tried to make a joke of it: I called her alternate persona, her not-quite-right alter ego, Sophisticated Lucy, the way people nickname enormous men Tiny. (Her other's defining characteristic was an eerie, plodding simplicity — a blunted lack of specificity.) She thought that was amusing, but her explanation for Sophisticated Lucy's intermittent appearance was "I'm running a start-up; I'm just exhausted."

I alternated between knowing (but not believing) that

she was lying and worrying that she was telling the truth and that something was terribly wrong with her. She must be having small strokes! What if she had a brain tumor? Or Lyme disease. And on top of all that she had to put up with me—treacherous me—accusing her of drinking when she was marshaling so much willpower to stay sober?

Battering her with questions about her drinking did not make me feel good. I felt cruel, abusive, but also paranoid, hysterical. I lived in a state of bewilderment punctuated by fury and aching guilt.

13

MONTHS INCHED BY LIKE THAT. AND THEN, SOMEHOW, THINGS got better.

We decided to get another cat—no, two! A pair of tiny, spotted sisters from an animal shelter on Long Island. We brought them home in a cardboard box punched with holes that they poked their noses through. They ran around the house curious, fearless, and then abruptly collapsed, always right next to each other. They did everything that way: They ate and drank in unison; they got in the litter box at the same time, like a two-headed kitten. Paolo would have sneered at their sweetness.

When Lucy was holding them, carefully clipping their nails, combing their fluff, she was the benevolent person I had met on the night of the blackout: Boy Scout Lady. She was the promise of family, decency, kin. And we were a kind of family now—they were only cats, but they were ours, new lives that we were taking on the care of, together. They slept in the bed with us and followed us around from room to room, except sometimes when we crossed paths with them and they looked at us as if they were seeing—for the first time in their lives—creatures so terrifying, so dangerous, they could barely stand to know that we existed. Then they went flying for the closets, where they hid until they were ready to recognize us again for who we were: the people who waited on them and met their every need. Their love slaves.

AN INVITATION CAME FROM ATHENS. My publisher there had decided for his own mysterious reasons to bring me over for a book tour during the worst of his country's economic crisis. I found myself catching a case of his optimism: So things have been horrible; they can always get better. Lucy decided to come, too.

When we got off the plane in Greece it was unseasonably warm. We stayed at the apartment of a friend of a friend, who was out of town, and there was something about it—the bed on the floor, the bathtub in the kitchen—that made us feel young and carefree. My publisher Dimitris took us out late at night to a *rebetika* club, a packed, smoky dance hall where men snapped their fingers as they spun in circles, and plates of lamb and eggplant kept arriving on the table in front of us. It was the kind of thing I always wish would happen but rarely does: We were brought into a private world and treated as if we belonged.

Dimitris's wife, Yiota, looked like a pretty, redheaded

Muppet. She told me about how she used to hang around Dimitris's bookshop when she was still married to her first husband. She had just given birth when she left to be with Dimitris. She smiled and shrugged and said, "People are not perfect."

One blue morning, Lucy and I took a ferry to an island called Aegina. We ate tiny fried fish off a waxed tablecloth in a café at the back of a marketplace, and men who looked like my grandfather stared at us. Stray cats ate our scraps. We walked through the alleyways in the pale winter light and talked about a drive we'd taken through Napa Valley eight years before, when we first got together. I'd been allergic to one of the wines and had hives on my eyelids and on the palms of my hands. Still, it was the happiest time, the most exciting. And now we had returned to each other.

Dimitris and Yiota cooked for us one night in their apartment, a cramped, rowdy place full of cigarette smoke, dolmades, children, and friends. "Americans are not relaxed," one of them told me, holding his three-year-old and drinking an ouzo. Greece was falling apart. The streets of Athens were crawling with cats and dogs that people had abandoned because they could no longer afford pet food. But our hosts were jubilant.

Their family didn't seem like a burden; it seemed like a party. The idea bloomed in my head that being ruled by something other than my own wishes and wanderlust might be a pleasure, a release.

———

IN THAT MAGIC ATHENIAN LIGHT, Lucy and I looked better to each other—not duplicitous, not drunk—*good* again. Our pure selves, redeemed. We had torn our marriage apart and put it back together, which meant that we were solid now, we decided. We would endure. Finally, I was eligible for motherhood. And I was thirty-seven.

We had several things going for us: shared values, dual incomes, extended family who lived nearby. We did not have any sperm, but that was not so hard to come by; you could buy it on the Internet, like everything else, and some people would just give it to you if you asked nicely. Lucy would be my co-parent, of course, but I wanted a man in our imaginary baby's life, too. When the kid asked, "Who's my dad?" I wanted to be able to answer with the name of a person whom he or she already knew and loved. Lucy and I both liked the idea of having another adult involved, who, we hoped, would want to spend the occasional weekend with his son or daughter, and could be an adjunct member of our family. We were intimidated by what we were taking on. We figured we could use all the help we could get. And pregnancy already seemed mysterious and unfathomable. I did not want a stranger's spawn growing inside of me.

On the morning we went to see the Acropolis, we started going through the attributes of all the potential donors we knew. One had a weak chin but an exceptional sense of humor, we agreed, as the sun climbed higher in the sky, and we took off our coats and hats in front of the Parthenon. Another was a talented athlete, but I worried about his temper. We climbed the narrow steps to the Temple of Athena, and I thought of my own father, who had loved to read to me from *Bulfinch's Mythology*, and gave Poseidon, Hera, and Zeus each a distinct voice.

It became obvious to whom we should turn. The boy who had fed us steak on his terrace on the night of the blackout—when we were innocents, before we'd done a single thing wrong—desperately wanted to be a parent, but a parent at a distance. He wanted the love without the labor. It was sort of perfect: from each according to his ability; to each according to his needs.

I excelled at nurturing, nagging, sterilizing germ-covered surfaces, and, so far as we knew, I had a working womb. Lucy was patient, good at math, an excellent driver, and handy. Our friend, who was delighted by the prospect of the kind of fatherhood we offered him when we got back to New York, was brilliant, shy, gentle, and, not insignificantly, rich. "I'll pay for college," he told us immediately. We did not argue.

For some time, my life had been an ugly, roiling mess, but I was going to pull it all together at the last minute. (It was better this way! I had acted out *before* I had children.) I had managed to solve the Jane Austen problems that women have been confronting for centuries—securing a provider for your children, finding a mate to pass the time with, and creating a convivial home—in an entirely unconventional way. I'd had to relinquish the poisonous heat of my affair, but with every day that felt like less of a sacrifice.

"People are not perfect," Yiota had said . . . and look at her. Bohemian but rooted, surrounded by children and cooking smells, out at all hours *with her husband,* drinking ouzo and watching plate-smashers dance. A spirited, sensuous matriarch who met human frailty with a redheaded shrug of broad-mindedness. The important thing was to love.

STILL, I WAS ANXIOUS when I went to the reproductive endocrinologist that spring. I lay back as he loaded our friend's spun sperm into a syringe, and I worried. I was so sick of failing at matrimony, I couldn't bear the idea of failing at maternity, too. I wondered if I was capable of the constancy I'd promised Lucy. I wondered if she was capable of the sobriety she'd promised me. And who would my child be? What murderous degenerate would I cook up in there? *(Would my baby be as bad as I was?)*

All of those thoughts dispersed when I rose from the table with the knowledge that I could be pregnant. Every night I fell asleep hoping. Every morning I woke up wondering. I had been equivocating for a decade and now that I had acted, it was suddenly clear: I couldn't wait to be a mother.

14

WE HAD GUESTS FOR THE FOURTH OF JULY, THE INAU-
guration of summer. We took them to the placid bay beach
on Shelter Island and to the shop down by the water where
you can eat sandwiches out back by the docks. I showed the
wife my tomatoes and she told me to glue pennies to the
stakes because copper repels snails.

Our friends left early Sunday morning to beat the traffic.
I went to my desk to do some work, and Lucy went out to
run errands. It was a hot day and I got up from the computer several times to take short, cold showers.

She was gone a long time. As it got later into the afternoon, my stomach began to twist.

When I finally heard Lucy turn onto the dirt road that
led to our house, I went out to the front yard. I watched her
tear into the driveway and stop the car abruptly, at a weird
angle. She opened the driver's-side door and nearly fell out.
I went and looked in the backseat and saw the cardboard

containers that had held two six-packs of beer. I counted the empty cans strewn on the floor: four, five, six . . . nine.

It is not a good feeling being right about something you have suspected when you finally gain undeniable confirmation that it's true. It is not the satisfying sensation of everything slipping into place for which you have yearned. It's more like, *Oh, right.* The man who has been staying over your whole life long is your mother's lover. The reason Lucy seems off sometimes is that she's still drinking. You have always known this. The only thing that's mysterious is how you managed to think it mysterious.

A pricking adrenaline went through me, as if I were witnessing a disaster in progress, a fire devouring the curtains, rather than the mundane reality of another person's inebriation. I felt myself departing, and my competent self taking over the controls.

I got the car keys from Lucy and told her it was time to take a nap—she fell asleep quickly in our bed. Then I found the kittens and my computer, and got in the Jeep, sweat rolling down the back of my neck, the insides of my thighs. I drove past the mariners' shops in Greenport and the stalwart farms and corny wineries of the North Fork. I looked at the people—from Guatemala, from Mexico—working in the fields, the sun pounding down on them indifferently. I wondered if everything that pained me would seem ridiculous to those women, or if some of our problems were the same. The cats roamed between the backseat and the passenger's side in front, pushing their faces toward the air conditioner.

It was the end of a holiday; the Long Island Expressway was smothered with traffic. We inched westward, and I told myself that this was simple: Get back to the city. Make more decisions later. *But what if Lucy really is an alcoholic? And what if I'm pregnant?* Either way, I told myself, you have to drive this car and park it.

It took hours, but finally I was creeping past the cemeteries of Queens, the rolling acres of bones. And then Lucy was calling my cellphone. "It's not your fault," she kept saying when I picked up. She was on the roof; she said that she was going to jump off. It wasn't my fault, but when she woke up and the house was empty, she felt that she was alone in the world and she wanted to die.

Cars honked and the cats howled as I pulled the Jeep onto the shoulder of the highway. I told her that dying was not an option. I told her she had to get down from the roof, now. Later, I would almost laugh out loud when I remembered telling her that we had two cats and she couldn't do this *to them*. I told her to go inside. I said it over and over again. I said it as many times as she said, "It's not your fault." I said, "We are going to hang up and then you are going to call me back from inside the house." I kept saying it until she agreed, and then I hung up the phone.

I called a friend of ours who I knew was on the island to ask her to go to our house, though we did not really know her well enough to ask for such a thing. But the phone just rang and rang and went to voicemail. I was sweating profusely; the cats were mewing in desperation. If I did nothing more, what would happen? Was there a real possibility that Lucy would hurt herself (that she would *kill* herself)? I thought: *We can't take that chance.* Then I called the police.

It all happened in seconds. I called 911 and got connected to the police department; I gave them my address and asked them to go to my house because a person there was threatening to commit suicide. Moments after I hung up, Lucy called back from inside and I wondered if I had just made a disastrous mistake.

But no. She was inside, but now she had a noose around her neck. (A *noose*? Where the hell had she gotten a noose?) She still wanted to die. Then she said she saw a police car pulling into our driveway and I told her that I had called them and she hung up the phone.

Our friend called back. I asked her to go to my house and see what she could do. Not much time passed—ten minutes? five?—before she called and said she was in my living room with the cops. But Lucy was gone.

She's dead. I felt my stomach falling through my body. *She has found a way to die.*

"No, no, wait," our friend was saying. "Hang on—they think they hear something in your bedroom, but they don't . . . oh. Yeah." They found Lucy sound asleep—snoring, in fact—on the floor under our bed.

———

THEY TOOK HER TO the emergency room in Greenport. She called me several hours later and said that she was all right, she was going to sleep. But at some point that night they moved her up to the psych ward, and nobody there would let me speak to her when I called the next morning; they wouldn't even confirm that she was there. "We're *married*," I kept saying, but they didn't care, or maybe it didn't matter. I was back in the car with the cats again, driving past the cemeteries and the Paris hotel, calling over and over, hoping I would get someone who would tell me something else. I felt as if I'd relinquished my child to the foster-care system in a moment of desperation and now I would never be able to get her back.

But eventually she called me herself, from a pay phone at the hospital. She did not sound like a child or a drunk or a person with a death wish. She sounded like my spouse. She said that it was awful; I had to get her out, *now.* She said to call her employees and tell them she'd had an accident, she was in the hospital, and then she gave me a complicated message to relay about a meeting with a client. I called her company. I called the hospital over and over until someone told me when there were visiting hours. I called and called and drove and drove until it occurred to me that wherever I drove and whomever I called, the truth would still be the same: My spouse, the person with whom I hoped to raise a child, was on the locked floor of a mental ward.

Finally, a doctor called me back—an articulate, straightforward woman who seemed competent and sane and who, I realized with wild relief, was now legally in charge of the situation. I asked her if she realized that my spouse was probably not really suicidal, that she was probably really an alcoholic. The doctor understood this. I asked why she was keeping Lucy in the hospital, then, and the psychiatrist said, "Because she needs to understand that her actions have consequences."

I was dazzled.

WHEN I FIRST SAW Lucy coming down the hall to greet me in the hospital, I was struck by how unmistakably I was still in love with her. I hadn't just ended up with her. I was not stuck with her. Here, humbled, in a pair of green hospital pajamas and the T-shirt she'd been wearing the last time I saw her, was the person I loved.

We sat on the burgundy couches in the lounge, where there were heaps of gummy old magazines on the end tables. "You won't like the selection," Lucy said. We could see the dark-blue Peconic Bay outside the windows, the sailboats floating off into the clouds on the horizon. Bleaching sun beat down on the black tar roofs of the other hospital buildings. I suggested that when this was all over, Lucy ought to try to sell them some solar panels.

Something had happened to her. She was back. "I guess the jury's in: I have a drinking problem," she said, which made us both laugh. That morning, when she woke up and saw where she was, she had been furious with me. She had eaten breakfast with people who were falling apart: schizophrenics who'd stopped taking their meds, people with the shakes still getting through the last stages of withdrawal. She was in the wrong place and I had put her there. But as the hours crawled by, she felt the resentment and resistance leaving her. *Of course* I'd called the police—what would it say if I hadn't? She'd started talking to people. For several hours, she was not ashamed. She did not feel better or worse than anyone else.

She pointed out a prim woman, who looked to be in her seventies, sitting on another sofa in the common room. She was addicted to painkillers, Lucy had learned in some kind of group therapy session they'd just had. This woman with stiffly styled white hair, wearing dainty navy flats, who looked like she might go to the same country club as Lucy's mother or attend meetings with her at the horticultural society, had kept a stockpile of pills hidden in a couch cushion. It was occurring to Lucy (to both of us) that there were other people (addicts) who looked fine but could not stop themselves from taking things that were warping their lives.

The doctors said Lucy had to stay one more night for observation. I was happy as I drove away toward the ferry, looking at the gardens glowing in the lambent afternoon light. Nature was thrumming with activity: insects, winding vines, bursting hollyhocks, all busy with the work of summer. Everything was growing.

The secret had been revealed, the mystery solved. I didn't need to convince Lucy or myself that this was an urgent problem. She would get help now. (Whatever that meant. I had no idea.) Things would soon be better.

When I got to the house, I cleaned the kitchen. I watched an episode of *30 Rock* on the computer while I made dinner out of what looked least old in the refrigerator. I went through the mail. Then I went to take the trash out to the shed in the backyard and saw that there was a noose still hanging from the oak tree.

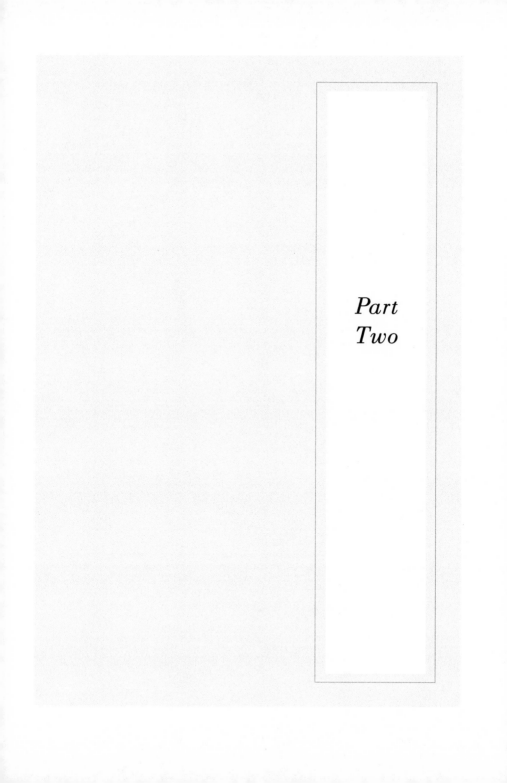

*Part
Two*

15

A MONTH LATER, I KNEW I WAS PREGNANT. I COULD SENSE it in every cell.

I called Emma, who'd recently gotten pregnant, and described how I felt: slightly sick, slightly insane, zooming with adrenaline. "Is it like you're receiving alien transmissions through your nipples?" Emma asked. I was. She told me to take a pregnancy test immediately.

Sweating, I charged up Amsterdam Avenue, looking for a pharmacy. After I'd bought a test, I found a Starbucks and stood in the sticky bathroom, overwhelmed by excitement and the mingling scents of urine and macchiato while I waited for the lines to appear in front of me on the little stick. And then there they were: plus.

It was like magic. A little eye of newt in my cauldron and suddenly I was a witch with the power to brew *life* into being. I called Lucy, but we kept getting disconnected. (She said she was in her office but it was noisy and chaotic in the background, and then she was gone, and when I called back it went straight to voicemail.) *But who cares? I'm pregnant!* It was much easier to reach my baby's father, who was in Japan for work but somehow immediately available, and overjoyed. We were both giddy, dazzled by what we'd done.

I called my own father, who yelped with delight. He said he couldn't believe he had a daughter who was old enough to be pregnant. I told him that, actually, he had a daughter who was *too* old to be pregnant, but somehow I'd managed it anyway. I would be turning thirty-eight soon. Getting pregnant felt like making it onto a plane the moment before the gate closes: You can't help but thrill.

Emma and I are exactly two months apart in age, and our children would be, too. We gushed about the matched set of playmates we were making. She was due in February, I'd give birth in April, when the fresh air blew in through the open windows.

My mother was happy in a way I never knew I could make her, and this made me love her with an openhearted abandon I had not experienced since childhood. It occurred to me that she was the one who had told me I could be the kind of woman who is free to do whatever she chooses. My mother had never once been surprised when I accomplished something. She had never believed me when I told her I would fail, even when she took me to the airport with my hulking backpack when I was twenty-two and afraid of Phnom Penh, afraid of Katmandu, and, of course, *so was she*. She didn't say, "You're right, it's too dangerous—let's go home."

She said, "Get on the plane. You'll be fine."

LUCY AND I FOUGHT less now. I was proud of her every time she ordered club soda at a restaurant. I had renewed hope in her business, her potential for success. Her human project.

But I never stopped worrying. I worried that she wasn't going to Alcoholics Anonymous meetings. (Though what did I know? Who was I to say that AA was the only way to be sober?) I worried about the dozens of non-alcoholic beers she consumed; the sight of a pile of empty cans made me edgy. I worried about how covert she was about her sobriety: She would let people pour wine in her glass and then just not drink it rather than admit she wasn't having any. (Why? Why wasn't she impressed with herself? I was! Why did we have a new secret to keep about alcohol?) I worried that there was something insufficiently ardent about her sobriety. But what?

NATURE DOES SOMETHING VERY shrewd to pregnant women. She makes them preoccupied with the babies inside of them so that by the time they give birth, they are already accustomed to being focused on their offspring, obsessed with their well-being, and so it is that infants survive. I was intent. *Who* was in there?

"At week seven your baby is the size of a blueberry," the woman in the video on the pregnancy website told me, "with dark spots that will become eyes." It seemed silly to be fixated on someone the size of a blueberry. But things were happening so fast! Just a few weeks later, I could hear the galloping heartbeat of the person inside me on a machine at the doctor's office.

I was meant to keep my obsession to myself, though—Lucy told me so, and the baby's father did, too. Miscarriages are common during the first trimester, and just think how awful it would be to tell people you were pregnant and then have to face them after everything ended in disappointment. But it was difficult. People would say, "What's new?" and it took all of my self-restraint not to reply, "Well, I'm cooking a human being inside my body. So there's that."

I pictured him shy and contemplative, a tiny human Ferdinand the Bull sitting under a cork tree in my stomach.

I WENT TO SAN DIEGO on Labor Day weekend to interview Lynn Vincent, a ghostwriter who had worked on Sarah Palin's memoir. I was expecting her to be strident, ignorant, nasty: my natural enemy. Instead she was fascinating. She told me about her harrowing childhood near Cape Canaveral, with an alcoholic mother who would lock her in the closet when she went down to the local bar—the Missile

Lounge, it was called. They were evicted from several places and eventually ended up living in a tent on the beach in Hawaii. Vincent ran away with nothing but a sundress and a bikini after she was attacked by her mother's boyfriend one afternoon when she was fifteen.

She took me to her favorite store in Old Town, where I saw something that made me weak: a blue-and-white Pendleton baby blanket with a whale leaping in the waves under a setting yellow sun. After I bought it, Vincent asked me if I had a friend who had just given birth. I couldn't hold it in. "No, *my* baby is going to lie on that blanket and look up at the oak trees this spring."

I knew Vincent was vehemently opposed to gay marriage and I waited for her to tell me that I had no right to be a mother. She looked like she was going to cry. "Oh, Ariel," she said. "How wonderful."

It seemed like the whole world was pleased for us, proud of me. *You're going to have a baby?* Yes, truly. A *living person* will be coming out of my body. I know it sounds ridiculous, but apparently that's just how this works.

Good tidings kept falling from the sky. At the twelve-week sonogram, Lucy and I gasped when we saw the baby on the monitor, flopping around like a fish—healthy, normal, *alive*. We both left the technician's office with a certainty that it was a boy, though we couldn't say why. A month later, I took a new blood test that read DNA in maternal plasma, and the results confirmed our hunch: It was a boy. And he had the right number of chromosomes.

I left a voicemail for Lucy's parents, telling them they would have another grandson soon. When they didn't return my call, I was crushed and angry and refused to be understanding when Lucy told me to think of the world they were raised in, and how far they'd come. My parents called every day: obsessed. I started exchanging letters with the parents of the baby's father. I was so excited when I received mail from them my hands would sometimes shake as I read. They were elderly and religious and lived far away but now we were kin. My son was drawing them toward me, a magnet for love.

We started to look for a bigger apartment. Lucy bought me white peaches at the farmers' market, because that was the only thing I felt like eating besides saltines. My friends asked me if I wanted games at my baby shower. (Definitely not.) Lucy's aunt Hope sent us a very small set of socks.

I felt less and less like a bad person. There was something so good inside of me—I was making something so good out of my very self—how rotten could I be? I started talking to the baby in my head instead of to myself. Even if you are not Robinson Crusoe in a solitary fort, as a human being you walk this world by yourself. But when you are pregnant, you are never alone.

AS MY HIPS WIDENED and my breasts grew turgid and tremendous, I felt myself turning into an animal, an actual biological creature ruled by my body, engrossed in its work.

I realized I was falling in some kind of hormonal love with my baby daddy. There was nothing romantic or sexual about it; it was much deeper. It was primal. I craved his presence. I wanted to look at his face and watch his hands move. We were out to lunch with him one day when I noticed I was sitting weirdly close to him in the booth, so that I could *smell* him. I knew that some miniature version of him would be coming out of me soon, and that I would love this person with a ferocity—a passion—that rendered all of my other emotions secondary.

This was not a fantastic feeling for Lucy. She felt demoted. She felt excluded. She started spending even more time than usual at work. (Though, oddly, it seemed like anytime I tried to call her at the office she was out, and her employees never knew where she had gone.) I remained anxious about her business, but it was a more detached concern now, because my baby was insulated by someone else's money: wealth, the world's greatest amniotic sac.

I RESERVED AN UGLY JEALOUSY for friends and acquaintances who came from rich families and never worried about their financial fate, for whom money was ultimately symbolic: They had careers and were glad to get paid, but what they were *really* living off was a pond of money that had been filling up for decades, in some cases generations. Their jobs were to some extent a matter of principle—one has to do *something*. Some of my female friends of this variety felt compelled to do something only until they had children. ("That *is* doing something!" Yes, of course it is. But it's something that a person can only do exclusively for a short period of time unless someone else is paying all the bills.)

I had gotten to a point where I could pay for myself. The idea of having financial responsibility for a child (to say nothing of the infuriating notion of having financial responsibility for Lucy if her business failed, when she was supposed to pay *for me*) had made me frantic. But now I was protected from all that! My baby's father was not only rich, but also self-made. (Not just wealth, but wealth I could respect.) He would pay for our child. There was no cause for fear. What's the worst that could happen—the baby needs the most expensive medicine in the world? *No problem.* To say that I was thankful for this security is to put it rather mildly.

Lucy resented my gratitude for the baby's father. She worried about her role in our family: "He's the father, you're the mother, what the hell am I?" I told her that, to the baby, she'd be the real parent—that at present, biology seemed like a big deal, but once our son was among us he would be closest to the people he lived with, his parents. His "dad" would really be like an uncle (a rich one) and *she* would be the point man. We'd even give the baby her last name!

But she yearned for the devotion she could already feel me directing toward my child, a devotion she had not experienced from me in years, if ever. She did not want the baby to be more important to me than she was.

"That's motherhood," I told her. "I have no choice."

16

IT WOULD BE AT LEAST A YEAR, MAYBE TWO, BEFORE I'D be able to leave home for weeks on end and feel the elation of a new place revealing itself to me. I wanted one last brush with freedom. I wanted to make one last offering to my career—the thing I'd made of which I was most proud, but not for long. My doctor told me that it was fine to fly up until the third trimester. When I was five months pregnant, I accepted an assignment in Mongolia.

Over a third of the country's population still lived nomadically, in felt tents, or *gers*, as they're called in Mongolia, herding sheep, goats, and horses on the steppes in the warmer months, almost exactly as their ancestors did. And yet Mongolia had attained an extraordinary level of advancement for women—the country beat Australia in the 2012 Gender Equity Index, I noticed, as I scrolled through the document on my computer at the office. Mongolia had vast supplies of coal, gold, and copper ore; its wealth was expected to double in five years. Ulaanbaatar, the capital city, already had a Louis Vuitton store not far from the *ger* camps where people gathered in winter, when the average temperature was negative thirteen degrees. Before the boom, Mongolia's best-known export was cashmere. As Jackson Cox, a young business consultant from Tennessee who lived in Ulaanbaatar, said when I called, "You're talking about an economy based on yak meat and goat hair." I would report on the country's impending transformation as money flooded in through the mining industry, and what it meant for women.

People were alarmed when I told them where I was going, but I liked the idea of being the kind of woman who'd go to the Gobi Desert pregnant, just as, when I was younger, I'd liked the idea of being the kind of girl who'd go to India by herself. I thought of Christiane Amanpour, pregnant at forty-one, flying off to Sarajevo to report on the war. I thought of a sunbaked blond documentarian in cargo pants with a bulging belly whom I'd just seen on television interviewing a woman in Mali who was also pregnant—they had smiled as they touched each other's stomachs.

"Are you insane?" my friend Ted asked when I told him about my upcoming trip.

"No, I'm rational," I replied, and thought, *But you aren't.* I am not superstitious and I'm not a sissy: If a doctor tells me there's nothing wrong with doing something, then I consider the matter settled. Lucy was the same way. If the baby's father felt any differently, he did not say so.

I observed among my peers a self-righteous sense of en-

titlement for the optimal pregnancy—prenatal acupunc-
ture, organic everything—that I found distasteful, the
antecedent to the frenzied efforts to transform a normal
home into a precious babyland. One *needs* a Diaper Genie,
a wipe warmer, a special changing table—no regular table
could possibly suffice!—a six-hundred-dollar stroller, a
BabyBjörn, a baby monitor, to say nothing of a night nurse
and a nanny. And yet women have been having babies since
the beginning of time without any of this and somehow the
species has endured.

So much of the panic around pregnancy seemed like
fussy yuppie nonsense. Secretly, I judged Emma for following all the rules so fastidiously, for getting edgy around deli
meat and treating coffee like crack rock. I would teach my
child the power of fearlessness. I would tell him, "When
you were inside of me, we went to see the edge of the earth."

I wasn't truly scared of anything but the Mongolian winter. The tourist season wound down in October, and by late
November, when I got on the plane, the nights were drop-
ping to twenty degrees below zero. But I was prepared: I'd
bought snow pants big enough to fit around my convex gut
and long underwear two sizes larger than normal.

To be pregnant is to be in some kind of discomfort pretty
much all the time. For the first few months, it was like waking up with a bad hangover every single morning but never
getting to drink—I felt nauseated but hungry, had a per-
petual headache, and was always desperate for a nap. That
had passed, but a week before I left for Mongolia I started

feeling an ache in my abdomen that was new. "Round-ligament pain" is what I heard from everyone I knew who'd been pregnant, and read on every prenatal website: the uterus expanding to accommodate the baby, as he finally grew big enough to make me look truly pregnant, instead of just chunky.

That thought comforted me on the fourteen-hour flight to Beijing, while I shifted endlessly in my seat, trying to find a position that didn't hurt my round ligaments.

WHEN MY CONNECTING FLIGHT landed in Mongolia, it was morning, but the icy gray haze made it look like dusk. Ulaanbaatar is among the most polluted capital cities in the world, as well as the coldest. The drive into town wound through frozen fields and clusters of gers, into a crowded city of stocky, Soviet-era municipal buildings, crisscrossing telephone and trolley lines, and old Tibetan Buddhist temples with pagoda roofs. The people on the streets moved quickly and clumsily, burdened with layers against the bitter weather.

I got together with Jackson Cox on my first night in town. He sent a chauffeured car to pick me up—every Westerner I met in UB had a car and driver—at the Blue Sky Hotel, a new and sharply pointed glass tower that split the cold sky like a shark fin. It was named for Tengri, god of the eternal blue sky, who was once worshipped by the Mongols, Turks, and Huns as the father of everything, along with Eje, mother earth. The hotel was across the street from Sükhbaatar Square, where young Mongolians had staged a hunger strike in the winter of 1990, waving banners with pictures of Genghis Khan and sleeping out in sub-zero temperatures, demanding the end of seventy years of Soviet control.

A decade later, Cox had come to UB with the International Republican Institute, an arm of the American political party that does development work in nations susceptible to capitalist influence. Cox was an earnest believer in the power of the free market, and by the time I met him, he was working as a liaison between foreign companies seeking to do business in Mongolia, and the country's parliament, the State Great Khural. Cox was gay, Southern, and progressive, though he still identified as a conservative because "those are my people," he told me, when I arrived at his apartment. He was listening to Beyoncé and pouring Champagne for a friend, a young mining-industry lawyer from New Jersey. His place was clean and modern, but modest: In UB, it's easier to accumulate wealth than it is to spend it.

The guys warned me that when I visited *gers* in the Gobi, I should expect to eat "the grossest food you've ever had in your life," as Cox's friend put it. "They bring out a bucket of meat that's been sitting there for a week, and they heat it up and think it's a scrumptious treat." I said that if I weren't pregnant I'd be all over it, but that I'd rather be thought rude than poison the baby. "How'd you get that baby?" Cox asked. I described the doctor's office, the blood tests, the syringe, and the moving being I'd seen on the computer screen. Cox said he wanted to be a parent someday, too.

We went to a French restaurant, where we all ordered beef—seafood is generally terrible in Mongolia, which is separated from the sea by its hulking neighbors, China and Russia—and then they took me to an underground gay bar called 100 Per Cent. It could have been in Brooklyn, except that everyone in Mongolia still smoked indoors. I liked sitting in a booth in a dark room full of Republicans and smoking gay Mongolians, but my body was feeling strange. I ended the night early.

WHEN I WOKE UP the next morning, the pain in my abdomen was insistent. I wondered if the baby was starting to kick, which everyone said would be happening soon. I called home, and Lucy told me to find a Western clinic, just in case, so I emailed Cox to get his doctor's phone number and scrawled it on my notepad. Then I went out to interview people: the minister of the environment; the president of a mining concern. There were local elections that day, and I went to some of the polling places with a Mongolian friend of Cox's to ask voters about their hopes for the boom.

My last meeting was with a herdsman and conservationist named Tsetsegee Munkhbayar, who had become a folk hero after he fired shots at a mining operation that was diverting water from nomadic communities. I met him in the sleek lobby of my hotel with Yondon Badral—a smart, sardonic man wearing jeans and a parka, whom I'd hired to translate for me in UB and then accompany me a few days later to the Gobi, where we'd drive a Land Rover across the cold sands to meet with miners and nomads. Munkhbayar was dressed in a long, traditional *deel* robe and a fur hat with a small metal falcon perched on top; he sat down in one of the Blue Sky's space station–style chairs. It was like having a latte with Kublai Khan.

In the middle of the interview, Badral stopped talking and looked at my face; I must have been showing my discomfort. He said that it was the same for his wife, who was also pregnant, just a few weeks further along than I was, and he explained the situation to Munkhbayar. The nomad's skin was chapped pink from the wind; his nostrils, eyes, and ears all looked as if they had receded into his face to escape the cold. I felt a little surge of pride when he said that I was brave to travel so far in my condition. But I was starting to worry.

I nearly canceled my second dinner with the Americans that evening, but they offered to meet me at the Japanese restaurant in my hotel and I figured that I needed to eat. Cox was leaving the next day to visit his family for Thanksgiving, and he was feeling guilty that he'd spent a fortune on a business-class ticket. I thought about my uncomfortable flight over and said that it was probably worth it. "You're being a princess," Cox's friend told him tartly, but I couldn't laugh. Something was happening inside me. I had to leave before the food came.

I ran back to my room, pulled off my pants, and squatted on the floor of the bathroom, just as I had in Cambodia when I had dysentery, a decade earlier. But the pain in that position was unbearable. I got on my knees and put my shoulders on the floor and pressed my cheek against the cool tile. I remember thinking, *This is going to be the craziest shit in history.*

I felt an unholy storm move through my body, and after that there is a brief lapse in my recollection; either I blacked out from the pain or I have blotted out the memory. And then there was another person on the floor in front of me, moving his arms and legs, *alive.* I heard myself say out loud, "This can't be good." But it looked good. My baby was as pretty as a seashell.

He was translucent and pink and very, very small, but he was flawless. His lovely lips were opening and closing, opening and closing, swallowing the new world. For a length of time I cannot delineate, I sat there, awestruck, transfixed. Every finger, every toenail, the golden shadow of his eyebrows coming in, the elegance of his shoulders— all of it was miraculous, astonishing. I held him up to my face, his head and shoulders filling my hand, his legs dangling almost to my elbow. I tried to think of something maternal I could do to convey to him that I was his mother, and that I had the situation completely under control. I kissed his forehead and his skin felt like a silky frog's on my mouth.

I was vaguely aware that there was an enormous volume of blood rushing out of me, and eventually that seemed interesting, too. I looked back and forth between my offspring and the lake of blood consuming the bathroom floor and I wondered what to do about the umbilical cord connecting those two sights. It was surprisingly thick and ghostly white, a twisted human rope. I felt sure that it needed to be severed—that's always the first thing that happens in the movies. I was afraid that if I didn't cut that cord my baby would somehow suffocate. I didn't have scissors. I yanked it out of myself with one swift, violent tug.

In my hand, his skin started to turn a soft shade of purple. I bled my way across the room to the phone and dialed the number for Cox's doctor I had scrawled on my reporting pad. I told the voice that answered that I had given birth in the Blue Sky Hotel and that I had been pregnant for nineteen weeks. The voice said that the baby would not live. "He's alive now," I said, looking at the person in my left hand. The voice said that he understood, but that it wouldn't last, and that he would send an ambulance for us immediately. I told him that if there was no chance the baby would make it I might as well take a cab. He said that that was not a good idea.

Before I put down my phone, I took a picture of my son. I worried that if I didn't I would never believe he had existed.

———

WHEN THE PAIR OF Mongolian EMTs came through the door, I stopped feeling competent and numb. One offered me a tampon, which I knew not to accept, but the realization that of the two of us I had more information stirred a sickening panic in me and I said I needed to throw up. She asked if I was drunk, and I said, offended, "No, I'm upset."

"Cry," she said. "You just cry, cry, cry." Her partner bent to insert a thick needle in my forearm and I wondered if it would give me Mongolian AIDS, but I felt unable to do anything but cry, cry, cry. She tried to take the baby from me, and I had an urge to bite her hand. As I lay on a gurney in the back of the ambulance with his body wrapped in a towel on top of my chest, I watched the frozen city flash by the windows. It occurred to me that perhaps I was going to go mad.

In the clinic, there were bright lights and more needles and IVs and I let go of the baby and that was the last I ever saw him. He was on one table and I was on another, far away, lying still under the screaming lights, and then, confusingly, the handsomest man in the world came through the door and said that he was my doctor. His voice sounded nice, familiar. I asked if he was South African. He was surprised I could tell, and I explained that I had spent time in his country, and then we talked a bit about the future of the ANC and how beautiful it is in Cape Town. I realized that I was covered in blood, sobbing, and flirting.

I borrowed the doctor's phone and called Lucy, who was sitting in the Jeep on the street in front of our apartment waiting for a parking spot. She wept and said that she would tell my parents and the baby's father—who, I felt sure, would never be able to forgive me, would never give me his sperm or his love or his money ever again.

It was very late when I handed the doctor back his phone. He said that he was going home, and that I could not return to the Blue Sky Hotel, where I might bleed to death in my room without anyone knowing. I stayed in the clinic overnight, wearing a T-shirt and an adult diaper that a kind, fat, giggling young nurse helped me into. Then she said, "You want toast and tea?" It was milky and sweet and reminded me of the chai I drank in the Himalayas, where I went so long ago, before I was old enough to worry about the expiration of my fertility. I had consumed a steady diet of hashish and Snickers in the mountains, and ended up in a blizzard that killed several hikers but somehow left me only chilly.

I had been so lucky. So little had truly gone wrong for me before that night on the bathroom floor. And I knew, as surely as I now knew that I wanted a child, that this change in fortune was my fault. I had boarded a plane out of vanity and selfishness, and the dark Mongolian sky had punished me. I was still a witch, but my powers were all gone.

That is not what Dr. John Gasson said when he came back to the clinic in the morning. He told me that I'd had a placental abruption, a very rare problem that, I later read, usually befalls women who are heavy cocaine users or who have high blood pressure. But sometimes it happens just because you're old. I could have been anywhere, he told me, and he repeated what he'd said the night before: There is no correlation between air travel and miscarriage. But he also asked, not unkindly, "So, at thirty-eight, you just decided to start a family?" I told him that was how we did it in Manhattan. Then I said that I needed to get out of the clinic in time for my eleven o'clock meeting with the secretary of the interior, whose office I arrived at promptly, after I went back to the Blue Sky and showered in my room, which looked like the site of a murder.

I spent the next five days in that room. Slowly, it set in that it was probably best if I went home instead of to the Gobi, but at first I could not leave. Thanksgiving came and went. There were rolling brownouts when everything went dark and still. I lay in my bed and ate Snickers and drank little bottles of whiskey from the minibar while I watched television programs that seemed as strange and bleak as my new life. Someone had put a white bath mat on top of the biggest bloodstain, the one next to the bed, where I had crouched when I called for help, and little by little the white went red and then brown as the blood seeped through it and oxidized.

I stared at it. I looked at the snow outside my window falling on the Soviet architecture. But mostly I looked at the picture of the baby.

17

WHEN I GOT BACK FROM MONGOLIA I WAS SO SAD I COULD barely breathe. I couldn't sleep. When I was alone, I made sounds that I never knew could come out of me.

"You'll have another one," my father told me, desperate, crying himself.

"No. I want *that* one." It was the savage truth. I had a longing—ferocious, primal, limitless, crazed—for the only person I had ever made. The sleeping almonds of his eyes. The graceful wings of his rib cage. His living, moving arms. *(His soul.)*

I had wanted to experience unconditional love, what Mary had described in Jerusalem: It is ordained; it can never be otherwise. A love that came from somewhere beyond my brain, beyond my ego. Here it was. A wild feeling from the deepest part of me, as deep and dark as the will to survive, for someone whom I alone had known during his whisper of a life. We were blood.

Grief is another world. Like the carnal world, it is one

where reason doesn't work. Logically, I knew that the person I'd lost was not fully formed, that he was the possibility of a person. But without him I was gutted. If my baby could not somehow be returned to me, nothing would ever be right again. This bitter winter would go on forever.

THERE WAS SOMETHING WRONG with the Lucy who'd picked me up at JFK. Her eyes were untenanted. But I couldn't stay focused on it because it was all just intolerable, everything. Late one night, I woke suddenly when I felt myself bleeding not just between my legs but also from my nipples. When I turned on the light I realized that it was milk, not blood, coming out of me.

It seemed like sadness was leaking out of me from every orifice. I cried ferociously and without warning—in bed, at the grocery store, sitting on the subway. I could not keep the story of what had happened inside my mouth. I went to buy clothes that would fit my big body but that didn't have bands of stretchy maternity elastic to accommodate a baby who wasn't there. I heard myself tell a horrified saleswoman, "I don't know what size I am, because I just had a baby. He died, but the good news is, now I'm fat."

On five or six occasions, I ran into mothers who had heard what had happened and they took one look at me and burst into tears. (Once, this happened with a man.) Well-meaning women would tell me, "I had a miscarriage, too," and I would reply, with unnerving intensity, "He was *alive."* Often, after I told them that, I tried to get them to look at the picture of the baby on my phone.

Of course, I was not supposed to say *the baby.* I wasn't supposed to even think it. He was not someone who slept and played; we did not have routines; he had not established preferences or facial expressions. But the statement *I had a miscarriage* did not feel like the truth. Euripides wrote, "What greater grief can there be for mortals than to see their children dead?" That was more like it.

Am I allowed to say "my son"? Was it not a statement of fact that I had given birth on the bathroom floor of the Blue Sky Hotel in Mongolia and watched my son live and die?

Everywhere I looked there were pregnant women, a gaudy show, repulsive.

TIME WOULD NOT MOVE. I thought of Simone de Beauvoir's novel *The Woman Destroyed.* "Has my watch stopped?" she wrote. "No. But its hands do not seem to be going around. Don't look at them. Think of something else — anything else; think of yesterday, a calm, ordinary, easy-flowing day, in spite of the nervous tension of waiting." There was no due date to anticipate now, but I was often distracted by a poisonous kind of counting: Seven days ago, he was still alive. Fifteen days ago, I saw him moving on the sonogram. (This went on for a very long time: Next month I would be giving birth. And later: He would be one week old now . . . six months . . . one year. *As I write this, he would be two and a half.*) I did nothing to stop the emails coming from the pregnancy website every Monday with news of what was happening in his development.

All roads led to my son. If I watched a movie with a little boy in it, I'd see shadows of where his face had been heading. If I walked along the icy Hudson I thought of how many layers he'd need to be out with me—a sweater, a bunting, *and* the blue whale blanket? I saw him under my closed eyelids like an imprint from the sun.

I WENT TO SEE DOCTORS, specialists, to get vial after vial of blood taken and tested. (Since that night at the clinic in Mongolia, the feeling of needles in my arms, the sight of my own blood flowing through thin tubes, had become routine.) They were checking to see if my placental abruption was due to a clotting problem, or perhaps a genetic predisposition.

It was crucial that I present a convincing simulacrum of sanity to the medical professionals: I mustn't cry or seem unhinged; I had to ask the questions that a rational person in my situation would want answered. Questions about cabin pressure, for example: If people get blood clots on long flights, couldn't a long flight upset the blood flow in the womb, in the placenta? It's not like that, they told me. People get blood clots on long flights from sitting for too long, not because they are in the sky.

Had I remembered to get up and stretch on the flight?

Of course I had. Like any pregnant woman, I'd had to use the bathroom every twenty minutes.

Could I ever have another baby? Yes, but the risk of miscarriage would now be increased. (I didn't see how it could be any higher than having *happened*.)

I went to see a bald, authoritative specialist in high-risk pregnancy at the Weill Cornell medical center who was not covered by my health insurance. I would pay anything; he was *the* expert, everybody said so—his word would be the last. He sat behind a long wooden desk, in front of a shelf of medical books. I liked that there were no photographs of people's babies up on the wall, no framed pictures of his own gleaming family on the desk. "There's no reason to think the same thing wouldn't have happened had you never left New York City," he told me after he reviewed my test results.

I nodded and tried to look competent, levelheaded, sharp—like someone he might be seated next to at a dinner party. But I wasn't really there to find out what had gone wrong. I did not care that my bloodwork had all come back normal. I didn't care that I was "perfectly fine." Secretly, I was still taking folic acid every day, just in case. And the only thing I wanted to learn was how to take what had happened and undo it. I knew I couldn't say it out loud, but I stared at the doctor and willed him to answer my question: *How do I get him back?*

18

LUCY—MY LUCY—WAS MISSING. FROM THE MOMENT SHE pulled up to the curb at Kennedy airport, I loathed the zombie who had swallowed my spouse. I realized she was long gone. Sometimes I would busy myself wondering whether she'd left me before or after I cheated on her. I could never really know, and it didn't matter now, but there were moments when considering it was a desirable break from thinking about the baby. When I slept, I dreamed of seashell lips and frozen skies.

How did people do this? People who'd lost children who had existed—not for minutes but for days, decades? Children who had voices, who had opened their eyes. Children with names. Did these people wake up every morning until the day they died and *beg* Mother Nature to return what she had given and then taken away?

One afternoon, one of Lucy's employees called to tell me that her staff wanted to have an intervention; they were all going to quit if she didn't get help. She had been drunk at a meeting—many meetings, in fact. I said that didn't make any sense: Lucy had been sober for more than five months. *She quit so I could get pregnant.* He said that he was sorry to be the one to tell me that that was not the case.

Three weeks after I returned from Mongolia, Lucy left for rehab.

For several days after she went away, I could not sleep in our bed. I went to Matt's apartment and told him that no, I did not want to sleep on the couch, and that I didn't want him to, either. I wanted to sleep next to him, where I could hear him breathing, so I would know that he hadn't disappeared into the darkness with my spouse and my son.

19

ALL OF MY CONJURING HAD LED ONLY TO RUIN AND DEATH. Now I was a wounded witch, wailing in the forest, undone.

There was an element of purity to the experience that I could almost appreciate. I didn't have to decide whether I wanted to be a mother. I didn't care about freedom or sexuality or marriage or monogamy. I didn't have to feel crazy when I couldn't make sense of where Lucy was or why she seemed off or why she was always in the basement for such a long time. The information was all in and it was all terrible and there was nothing to be done to fix any of it. My competent self—so strong, *since childhood*, so perspicacious, always looking for opportunities, adventures, glory, always trying to protect me from defeat—had been crushed. The wide-open blue forever had spoken: You control *nothing*.

I HAD RECEIVED A beautiful email from the baby's father when I was still in Mongolia. Nature is wasteful, he had said. That's why there are so many pinecones on the forest floor—his mother had pointed them out to him once when he was a child, and explained that nature starts many more projects than she can ever finish.

At first, he wanted to try again. But then he didn't. And then my downfall was complete.

When I got on the plane to Mongolia, I was pregnant, living with my spouse, moving to a lovely apartment, and financially insulated by a wealthy man. A month later, none of that was true. Instead, I was thirty-eight, childless, alone, emotionally and monetarily unprepared to be a single mother. I'd become a cautionary tale, like the women Elizabeth Hardwick described in *Sleepless Nights,* who "wander about in their dreadful freedom like old oxen left behind, totally unprovided for."

My pristine grief was intermittently marred by dread. I thought of the chilling words a friend of mine had once used to explain why his older sister had married a man she did not love when she was reaching the end of her childbearing years: She had run out of runway.

At night I sat on my couch and sobbed so hard I screamed—on the couch the baby's father and I had picked out together at a fancy store after I got my first book deal, when we were just becoming friends. When I was young. When I had no idea that all over the city, all over the world, there were people walking around sealed in their own universes of loss, independent solar systems of suffering closed off from the regular world, where things make sense and language is all you need to tell the truth.

GRIEF IS A WORLD you walk through skinned, unshelled. A person would speak to me unkindly—or even ungently—on the street or in an elevator, and I would feel myself ripping apart, the membrane of normalcy I'd pulled on to leave the house coming undone. Better to stay inside my snug apartment, alone with the cats, where I didn't have to pretend to be intact.

My bedroom was taken up almost entirely by the bed and two drafty windows. It was like a ship bunk: In there, I was sailing out over the trees and rooftops of Chelsea through the purple dawn, into the cold night sky. Or at midday, after a vague fit of sleep, I would be called up on deck by the sound of children screeching with pleasure across the street in Clement Clarke Moore Park. Noon would become four in the afternoon; four in the afternoon would become four in the morning. The flow of blood, the draining and filling of the sky with light.

There was a long hallway connecting that room to the living room and my tiny kitchen, and I would throw balls and toys back and forth for the cats to chase. *Thank God for the cats*, I thought, when they had the compassion to sleep next to me on the couch, or looked on curious but unfazed as I bawled. They were good companions to have in this strange new world of grief: nonverbal, affectionate, no more baffled by agony than they were by dishwashing.

MY MOTHER CAME TO stay with me. We ordered spring rolls and Buddha's Delight. When I asked her, "What will become of me?" she said, "You will be fine." Sometimes she said, "You are not alone."

She slept next to me in her green flowered nightgown, one of the few she could find that had no seams in places that rubbed against the itchy scars that divided her torso into different districts: the buckled skin up north where there used to be two mountainous breasts; the slashed stomach where they took fat and tissue to reconstruct my mother's left breast after her first mastectomy followed her first cancer. Several years later, they found a second cancer in her right breast, and my mother demanded that they remove both breasts, once and for all. She did not have them reconstructed. She'd had enough of hospitals at that point. She used to have two breasts and two lives; she used to seem unknowable. Life had eroded her body, her restlessness, her expectations, and left her somehow gentle and content.

I was in my late twenties when she had her first cancer and my early thirties when she had her second. I was scared and sad and rattled both times. But I had not really allowed myself to contemplate what it felt like to be her, fighting death, as a single woman turning sixty, and then living with chronic pain and a body transformed by amputations. Since puberty, she had been aware of people's (men's) eyes on her breasts, taking in the remarkable size of them. Now she noticed their eyes taking in the remarkable absence.

She had her own pain. She had her own reasons. That was something I never saw clearly before motherhood flashed in front of my eyes, impairing and intensifying my vision. Nothing has looked entirely the same since.

20

I PACKED LUCY'S THINGS CAREFULLY INTO THE CORRU-
gated cardboard boxes in which my warm leggings and
special gloves for Mongolia had arrived weeks earlier from
L.L.Bean. Part of me was tender as I contemplated which
T-shirt, which pajamas, would be the most comforting for
her to have at rehab. She should have her sneakers in case
she wanted to start running again—which would be
healthy, good for her. If Lucy could get back into athleti-
cism maybe she'd have something to focus on and it would
help. She would need sports bras and shorts, track pants
and tube socks, which I rolled into tight little balls. She
would want to look put together, too; keeping up appear-
ances mattered to her. I packed her good suede shoes and
her gray cashmere sweater. I folded her favorite jeans and
packed them next to the blue plaid shirt I'd gotten her for
Christmas one year, comfortable but sharp. She had been
so happy when she unwrapped it—Lucy was the easiest

person to shop for. Anything that would look good on a teddy bear appealed to her: She could never have enough corduroy or gingham.

But then it was only a false front, wasn't it—her wholesomeness, her reliability.

The audacity of her disintegrating at this moment. *How could you do this to me?* The mounting horror of her debts—loans I had been unaware of, the cost of her treatment. *It was your job to make me safe.* The obvious necessity to sell the house on Shelter Island to pay for everything. *Is nothing mine in this world?* The indignity of an addiction counselor at her rehab—a stranger!—informing me that I should not call my spouse to demand the truth when lies unfurled themselves in my head: It was not what Lucy needed.

What she needs? She's the one we're worried about? What does a girl have to do to be the victim around here?

How dare she have been drinking all this time when she swore she was sober. I'd been sick with guilt about my affair for two years and all the while she was lying about this? I told her—many times—"I feel *insane.*" And she never said, "You're not crazy. You're right."

I took the framed pictures of us off the wall and put them in a drawer. I spread my clothes out in both of our closets with abandon. I taped the box of her things closed and mailed it away.

Part of me just wanted her shit out of my house.

———

I HAVE NEVER BEEN much good at making things up. I was good at seeing what was in front of my face and deciding what it meant, then writing about it so that others were swayed by my perception. How had I failed to perceive that Lucy had never stopped drinking? There had been a hundred shadows of her alcoholism. The empty beer cans I found—preposterously—wedged between the sink and the radiator in the bathroom on Shelter Island just a few days after I got home from Mongolia. ("Those must have been there from before I quit drinking," she had said.) Where *was* she all the time? Why was she always tired, lying down to nap on the couch in the middle of dinner at a friend's house? Why did her personality seem subtly but insistently tweaked half the time when she got home from work?

Only much later did I see that it had never mattered which questions I had asked her or how shrewdly I had scrutinized her answers. Addicts *lie*. (This should not have been so difficult for me to understand: When I was addicted to lust, I lied all the time, sometimes to cover my tracks, and sometimes purely out of habit.)

But whatever I had failed to comprehend about Lucy's drinking was incidental, was nothing. How had I failed to perceive what was obvious to everyone else? *You don't fly to Mongolia pregnant.*

21

MY FRIEND DAVID KLAGSBRUN, WHO GREW UP AROUND the corner from me in Larchmont, was turning forty that winter, and Matt and I drove up for his party in Katonah, where David lived with his wife and two young sons. It was good to be back in a car with Matt, the way we used to be all the time.

The summer after our freshman year of college, I worked at a French restaurant in Larchmont and Matt sold a cleaning powder for septic tanks. In the evenings after dinner he would pick me up in his gray car at my mother's house, and I'd roll us a joint—"Don't make it too tight, Ar," he'd say every time, and every time I'd say, "I *got* it," and almost every time I would roll too tightly—and we would smoke it as we drove past David Klagsbrun's house, past the parochial school on Weaver Street that looked like a fire station, over the bridge near the turnoff for that ersatz Hebrew school where I went when I demanded a bat mitzvah because everybody else was having one (and where once, when I was playing Tzeitel in our production of *Fiddler on the Roof*, I argued with the teacher about a dramatic point and he said, exasperated, "Do you want to direct this yourself?" And I said, "God, *yes*"). Then we'd coast into the Manor, the section of town with yards like parks and the kind of houses that make you stare with longing even when you are nineteen years old, as we were, and want nothing more than to get the hell out of the suburbs.

There was the green Victorian with the great, peaceful porch; the Gothic-y Tudor that was Matt's favorite; the sprawling white Mediterranean with concave red tiles mounded on the roof and a huge greenhouse on one side that I wished was mine. We would drift around in the quiet, leafy dark, gazing stoned and acquisitive at the houses, the hundred-year-old oak trees, the blinking green Gatsby lights out on Long Island somewhere across the sloshing sea. And it all felt like ours because we were in college now, and didn't really live there anymore. We used to belong to that town, to be stuck there, but it had become our nighttime playground, a movie for us to drive around in.

We were saving up that summer to go on a road trip to California. "California, Max!" we'd say, quoting Tony Roberts in *Annie Hall*. We left in mid-August with six hundred dollars each and drove for days through the endless spread of Pennsylvania and Ohio, the juicy green of Kansas. But we never felt cooped up. The car was our spaceship: We felt that inside of it, we experienced a different air pressure from everybody else.

"I'm Lester the Nightfly / Hello Baton Rouge!" Donald Fagen sang on the car stereo. We talked about Matt's brother, my parents, Emma, David Klagsbrun. Or jazz: Matt was always pleased if I could identify Sarah Vaughan's voice on a song—he told me that when people say, "It sounds like Ella," it means they know nothing, they are basically saying, "It tastes like chicken." We were both into short stories that summer, so we talked about Lorrie Moore, J. D. Salinger, Raymond Carver, Mary Gaitskill. That often spilled over into the main topic: who we were going to be when we grew up.

I loved driving late at night when Matt was asleep in the passenger seat and I became all-powerful, immortal, with no need for sleep or food or conversation. I needed only gas and road, which went on and on, through the dark, through the rain and heat lightning, through the mountains and the sky. I remember the violet morning we crossed into Utah, and in the gathering light I could see that the land along the roadside was all white, though it was much too hot for snow. Matt woke up when I pulled over, and we got out to walk on the crunching mineral crust of the Great Salt Lake Desert, miles of shiny whiteness.

A day later when we were coming into California it was very hot on the highway and we saw a little lake. We didn't know if it was a reservoir or a pond or what, but we knew that it was ours. We parked and ran across the highway and took off our clothes and jumped in and the water was just the right cold, it smelled pure and perfect, and *this* was what we'd been waiting for our entire childhoods. There was no lunch or dinner, there was no job or school, there were no bathing suits or rules.

IN KATONAH, AT DAVID KLAGSBRUN'S fortieth birthday dinner, we met his new suburban friends. They were different from us, Matt and I felt, more grown-up (less fun). I made small talk on the cold front deck of the restaurant with a curly-haired woman, and she told me about her daughters and how exhausted she was all the time, and then something turned in her head and her face looked like it wasn't sure what to do with itself. She said, "Are you the Ariel who all the bad things happened to?"

I said that I was, and wondered how many other Ariels she could possibly have to choose from.

She said, "Everything happens for a reason."

Technically, that is a statement of fact. The reason I was talking to that woman was that she was friends with David. The reason she was friends with David was that he'd moved to the suburbs, where he didn't know anyone. The reason he didn't know anyone was that his best friends (his *real* friends) had grown up with him in those same suburbs and vowed never to return, because even though Westchester is tranquil and wonderfully vegetated, there is an empty stillness that falls there every day from New Year's until the crocuses come up that can suck the joy right out of life. Was that what she meant?

I told the others about that conversation the next morning and we couldn't stop riffing on it. The reason Matt was horny was that he hadn't had sex in months. The reason he hadn't was that every time he went on an Internet date, he found himself too worried about the inevitable breakup he'd have to initiate to initiate the sex that could precede it. David's six-year-old came in from the yard, and he got in on it, too: The reason he was drinking juice was that he was thirsty. The reason he was thirsty was that he'd been running around with his brother, still in his footie pajamas (which also happened to be the reason that there was mud, everywhere). It was clear: Everything happens for at least one reason.

It was fun. Sort of. The reason it was only sort of fun was that my life had collapsed. Unlike the people at the party, with their homes full of spouses and children, I was as alone and unmoored as I'd been twenty years ago, in these same suburbs, hanging out with the same boys. In the intervening decades, I'd thought I was going somewhere. But I had just been driving around.

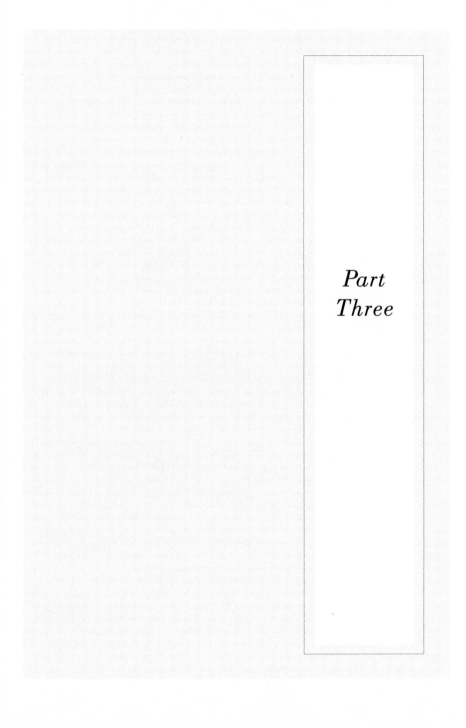

*Part
Three*

22

AN EMAIL ARRIVES FROM DR. JOHN GASSON, MEDICAL
Director, SOS International Clinic, Ulaanbaatar. As promised, he has sent my medical report, which I need to submit
to my insurance company. He has also attached a study on
preterm birth that he mentioned when we were in the
clinic. "Just in case you have any lingering doubt or feelings
of guilt," he writes.

I ask him if it is normal that I'm lactating. He explains
that the oxytocin that brings on contractions also signals the
body to lactate. He adds that the "milk letdown reflex after
a miscarriage is one of nature's less kind tricks," which I
think is an elegant and apt way of putting it.

Dr. John asks how I am feeling. I tell him that I am in
hell. But the very fact of him asking, of being in communi-
cation with the person who was there that night, is a balm
beyond any other.

I thank him for asking. I thank him for being so kind to
me at the clinic. I ask if it's gotten even colder in UB. He

says that it has, but that the real problem is the pollution: The colder it gets, the more garbage and coal people burn in the streets for warmth and the harder it becomes to breathe.

He is in UB only half the time. He explains that six months of the year, he lives on the other side of the world in South Africa, in a cottage he built himself. There is a stable there that he put up for his horses, and next door, his two teenagers live with their mother and her second husband. When Dr. John is at home, he goes surfing early in the morning with his seventeen-year-old, and riding in the afternoon with his younger son when he gets home from school. "I do miss my kids and horses when I am away and that can be difficult," he writes. "The kids will be leaving school soon and off to university. Then I will just have the horses to miss."

I tell him about the time I spent in Cape Town, about my Ethiopian driver, Zerihun, and how we walked up Table Mountain together when we had time between interviews. I describe the meeting with the track team out in the wind in Limpopo, the encounter in Pretoria with Caster Semenya.

Actually, he knows that story: He has been reading some of my articles online. He says he likes the way I write.

I like the way that he writes, too: "One of my father's better stories involved being woken up in the early hours of the morning and leaving in some haste as the house was burning. He remembers himself and his younger brother peering through the back window of the motorcar, still in their Victorian nightdresses, as the night sky lit up over the rapidly receding town of Barberton. The veracity of his account is suspect, but what is fact is that some very incriminating documents conveniently disappeared in the fire. My grandfather was an Irish lawyer of highly suspect morals, and the family is convinced that my grandmother took responsibility for clearing his tracks. She left him frequently, but remarried him on three separate occasions, so he obviously had some charm when not in jail." His sentences are so jaunty! And so foreign. They sound like they were written in not just another place but another time. His stories transport me.

Dr. John tells me about his childhood in Zambia and Zimbabwe—Rhodesia, to him, at the time. Growing up, he didn't question why, if they were Englishmen, as the people they socialized with considered themselves to be, they lived in a country where everyone else spoke Shona and Ndebele. He did not really contemplate what it meant that his father—also a doctor—and his grandfather before him were colonialists, until many years later, when he began to question everything he'd been taught about blackness, whiteness, and where he belonged. As a teenager, he just thought Africa was home.

He tells me about the time he flipped his brother's car on the way back from the Chimanimani mountains when they were still in high school, and then they snuck into a hotel in Bulawayo, took a bath, and hitched home, clean and delighted with their ingenuity, arriving just before curfew. His brother, Greg, was his best friend growing up; they were only two years apart in age. Their mother died when they were toddlers. Greg died, too, in a motorcycle accident when he was twenty-one. I can feel how haunted Dr. John Gasson was—is—by that loss from six thousand miles away. His mother, his brother, his father, his country, no longer exist, are part of the past.

When we converse in writing, everything feels complete, discrete. I don't have to explain what just happened; he was there. Unlike the rest of the people in my life, he never knew Lucy, never knew me as half of a couple, so when we are communicating I feel that lack somewhat less. Within the confines of our epistolary friendship, I am not missing pieces of my life—except the one that came from my own body, the one that Dr. John alone has seen. Not a picture of the piece, the person.

I wonder sometimes if my grief is disproportionate, inappropriate. "I saw my father fall apart after my brother got killed," Dr. John tells me. "But he had the consolation of knowing the adult that my brother briefly became. You don't even know what your son would have been like as a little boy. I feel desperately sorry for you."

Only Dr. John saw him, and only Dr. John saw me with him. Only Dr. John saw what feels so violently true to me I can't stand that it is invisible to everybody else on earth: *Here is a mother with her baby who has died.*

And so, in one way, our friendship is a kind of fiction.

We are two people on opposite ends of the earth, who do not know each other, who write each other emails as if we are familiars. (At first, we just exchange a few, here and there. But soon we are writing regularly. And the first thing I do when I wake up after I stop crying is check to see if he has sent me an email full of stories about places I have never seen, in a voice that is swashbuckling but somehow intimate.) In another way, these emails—and that picture— are the only things that are real to me.

23

NEW YORK CITY IS COLD and elegant and the white lights on the stone buildings are like jewelry on a stately dame. Matt stays on my couch. I make my mother's chicken cutlets, we watch *Seinfeld* reruns and pay-per-view, and I cry in the shower.

"Should I go get more wine?" Matt asks periodically.

"Sure," I tell him. "*I'm* not an alcoholic. And I'm not pregnant, either."

On Christmas Eve, I wear the only dress that fits and take Matt to a party at the writer Gay Talese's townhouse. At least a hundred people have come, and they wear pearls and red lipstick or good suits; there are waiters in black bowties forking slices of pink steak onto plates. Talese is shaking hands with Mayor Bloomberg, two white-haired men pleased with their stations, satisfied with their New York lives.

At the previous year's party, Lucy and I had talked to Nora Ephron, whom I'd once profiled for *The New Yorker*.

"I have a huge number of friends who've managed to change their lives," Ephron told me the first time I interviewed her. "Women way more than men. It's sort of the silver lining of things not being quite fair: It's not as big a deal if you say, 'I'm going to take a salary cut and see if I can be something else . . . a nightclub singer.'" She had changed her own life, transforming herself from a journalist into perhaps the most successful female director in Hollywood, after Carl Bernstein notoriously cheated on her while she was pregnant and their marriage dissolved. ("Everything is copy," she said.)

Ephron was opposed to whining. She told me she did not believe in it. "I don't mean that you can't sit at home and feel sorry for yourself—*briefly*," she said one afternoon when we were sitting on her couch, watching the sun set behind the Chrysler Building out her living room window. "But then I think you have to just start typing and do the next thing." She must have known she was dying when she said that. She passed away a few weeks before I got pregnant.

I notice her son and her widower coming in the Taleseses' front door as Matt goes off to find Champagne. They look like I do: blown apart. I wonder if they whine about losing Nora now that she isn't around to scold them for it.

After we've eaten dinner, Matt suggests we take a taxi up to the Carlyle: "We're dressed for it," he says, shrugging. We do, and order Manhattans at Bemelmans Bar, where the ceiling is covered in gold leaf and the walls are painted with murals of French parks and Madeline lining up with her playmates in front of a smiling nun. We listen to the jazz trio (I think they're really good; Matt says, "Tastes like chicken") but also we talk and talk and make each other laugh the way we've been able to since we were fourteen years old—hard enough to beg the other person to shut up. There are jewel-like moments when I experience gratitude.

When we get back to the apartment, I beg Matt to put on some enormous pink pajamas with daisies all over them that my stepmother sent me for Hanukkah: "Come on— I've been through so much!" Eventually he gets into them, and then does the hora around my coffee table for a while. I feel less alone than I have in months.

For some reason, I still have Matt. I still have Emma. I still have New York, and I am still a writer.

And the truth is, the ten or twenty minutes I was somebody's mother were black magic. There is nothing I would trade them for. There is no place I would rather have seen.

24

I GO TO VISIT LUCY IN REHAB. WE SIT IN AN AIRLESS OFFICE
with one of her counselors, who uses words strangely: Instead of "living with guilt," she says "living *in* guilt"; instead of "drinking," she says "using." The woman urges me
to go to Al-Anon—which sounds like something from Sci-
entology, but also like Arabic. (And why do *I* have to go
anywhere? I'm not the one with the problem.) The room
we are in is very small; the window—which is sealed shut
like they are in hotel rooms now—overlooks an empty
parking lot.

Lucy is wearing the clothes that I sent her. She looks
clean and a little tan and she smells like sunscreen and
laundry soap. I want to touch her head, push her tawny hair
behind her ears. Also I want to slap her.

I ask about times I suspected she was drinking, and she
tells me that invariably yes, she was, and actually it was
much worse than that. It was every day, sometimes starting

at a bar in the morning before work. She describes a ruthless craving that was with her all the time. She would try to placate it just enough, but not so much that anyone would notice. It was an exhausting and isolating task from which she had no respite.

I am unpleasantly surprised to feel not the anger or the sense of betrayal I've been cultivating, but an awful empathy: How lonely this must have been for her. While I was emailing the baby's father about names, decorating the new apartment in my head, Lucy had been enslaved. And she couldn't tell me.

I think of pictures of Lucy from her childhood: freckled, scampish, radiant. Standing in front of Mount Rushmore in black and white, five years old, wearing cowboy boots. A little older, attempting a plié in a ridiculous pink tutu, compromised but game. In the photograph that I always kept on my bedside until I stuffed it in the drawer after she left, she couldn't have been more than one, she barely had hair. But it was already Lucy: that smile straight from the sun. I have an excruciating wish that she would age backward, into a baby, so that I could raise her now. So I could forgive her everything, anything, and love her with all the violence in my heart, and none of the need.

The counselor says that we are "at the beginning of a long, uphill journey." She says, "Relapse is a part of recovery."

I think, *You have got to be fucking kidding me.*

I say, "Do I look like someone who's ready for a long, uphill journey?" Lucy snickers for a second, and I love her. I love her much more than I want to.

But I am worn down and out. The thought of another trip crushes me. I tell Lucy, You are my family. But I'm not coming with you.

25

FOR A WHILE, SHE STOPS SPEAKING TO ME AND I DON'T think that I can bear it. I feel severed and deprived, though I'm the one who said I wanted out.

But not like this! Wasn't I still entitled to her friendship? Her love? After *ten years*? I call her old friend DJ and beg him for information about Lucy—how she's doing, what she's thinking. I plead my case: I warned her over and over again that eventually there would come a time when I would be unable to refill the tank of hope and credulity. *She* has made this happen, not me!

DJ thinks this is good for her. If she has to cut me out of her life in order to get well, then that's exactly what she should be doing. He tells me I need to find a way to accept it, for my own sanity as much as hers.

He seems uncharacteristically sure of what he's saying. But I do manage to make him cry.

———

IN DESPERATION, I GO to an Al-Anon meeting. It is on the second floor of a church rectory, in a room with green-and-white tiles on the floor and rectangular fluorescent lights vibrating on the ceiling. There is a table with leaflets and brochures; I take a bookmark that has a list of "Dos" on the front and "Don'ts" on the back. Then I join the dozen or so people sitting in a circle in the kind of chairs we had in school, the ones with imitation wood trays attached on the right side, in lieu of desks.

A guy in his thirties reads something procedural from a shabby binder to start the meeting—"We have no dues or fees but we do have expenses"—and then says it's time for the "qualification." It's confusing: It becomes clear that a qualification is a speech, because now a woman named Mallory who could be twenty-nine or fifty-two is telling us about her experience growing up with an alcoholic mother, whom she identifies as her first "qualifier." (If alcoholics are addicted to drinking, it seems clear that these people are addicted to repurposing the word *qualify*.) Mallory says she was raised never to speak about her feelings, never to express "the holy trinity of shame, anger, and fear."

I'm in the wrong place. My parents never drank, and I've never *stopped* verbalizing my feelings. I have nothing in common with these people, and I dislike their awkward pidgin.

I look at the clock. I have been here for five minutes,

tops. I wonder if there's a way I could find anyone in the school-chair circle attractive. (There isn't.) I read the list on the back of the bookmark.

Don't:

> Be self-righteous.
> Try to dominate, nag, scold, or complain.
> Lose your temper.
> Try to push anyone but yourself.
> Keep bringing up the past.
> Keep checking up on the alcoholic.
> Wallow in self-pity.
> Make threats you don't intend to carry out.
> Be overprotective.
> Be a doormat.

It is, I think, too bad that's not the "Do" list, because then I would score a perfect ten.

Mallory has been feeling "very triggered" this week. Her ex-husband—her "second qualifier"—has been inconsistent in their negotiations about who should get to spend midwinter vacation with their daughter, and inconsistent is one of "the four I's." The other three are *irrational, isolating,* and *in denial,* and apparently if an addict is exhibiting these I's routinely, it means he or she is "active" (which is to say "using," which is to say—as we do in America—*drinking*). "And do you know what 'denial' stands for?" Mallory adopts a knowing smirk, and pauses for effect. "'Don't Even Know I Am Lying.'" Several people issue world-weary grunts of acknowledgment. I resist the urge to point out that this kind of "know" doesn't start with *n*.

Mallory smiles even more sagely and tells us that "in the rooms," she's learned to "keep the focus on myself," and not to obsess about her ex-husband's drinking. She has learned to take it one day at a time, and to have faith that "wherever I am today is exactly where I need to be," because of a "program called Al-Anon."

My head is about to explode. Why did Mallory not just say "Al-Anon"? We all know it's "a program"—we're fucking *here*, right now. Why the phrase "in the rooms," when the perfectly normal "at meetings" already exists in English? Why all this mysterious, ridiculous qualifying, and why this reluctance to say "drinking" when we're all here because of it?

"Hi, I'm Jason, and I'm grateful to be here," says a man to my left, who still has on his overcoat; he is probably on his lunch break from an office job in the area.

"Hi, Jason."

Jason thanks Mallory for her qualification and tells her that he appreciates her serenity and that he can relate to her experience. "The thing about denial," he says, "is that it's like sleeping: You don't know you're doing it when you're doing it."

There is an extravagantly loud, knowing grunt in response, and I am aghast to realize that I am its source. *Beer cans crumpled between the sink and the radiator.* Why did I ask for an explanation when I saw them there, instead of just recognizing what they were: *proof?* It seems so preposterous—so funny, really—to think that I was forever worried that Lucy had a brain tumor, Lyme disease, a thyroid problem, a vitamin deficiency. Exactly how deluded would you have to be to live with someone, to sleep with her every night, and convince yourself that she was sober when she was drinking, using, whatever, every single day?

A younger woman goes next. She is in her early twenties, her hair is a streaky, mousy blond, she wears a skirt and tights and a fuzzy white sweater. There is a trace of something Eastern European in her voice, but it's hard to pin down because she starts to cry almost as soon as she speaks. She moved here with her boyfriend several years ago; at first it was wonderful, like no home she'd ever known. Now she comes home from work expecting to see *him*, looking forward to his company, but instead *drunk him* is there, and as soon as she sees who it is, she's furious, and somehow shocked, even though it's a regular occurrence. Invariably, he denies that he's been drinking; he tells her he feels harassed and monitored—that her accusations make him feel like he might as well drink, because he's getting so much grief about it.

She worries he will get fired. She misses his attention. She gets her hopes up that things will change, and they do for a while, but then *drunk him* comes back, just when she's starting to forget he exists.

"I'm not a mean person," she says, wiping her eyes with the back of her hand. But she is mean to her boyfriend when she thinks he's drunk. Sometimes she insults him, calls him pathetic. (*You're the worst*, I said. And I remember the look on Lucy's face.) She worries she's not a loving person. She feels bewildered and angry and guilty, but most of all she feels insane.

When she finishes, several people say, "Keep coming back," in unison. But that's it. They don't give her advice or respond to what she's just said, even though her face is mottled pink and her breathing is jagged.

"I'm grateful to be here," Gavin, an older black man who is wearing a sweater vest, tells the group. I realize that I am grateful to be here, too. I'm grateful not to be yelling at Sophisticated Lucy, or to be feeling like a bad person for having just yelled at her. I'm grateful I'm not tormented by whether I'm crazy or whether I'm right. I'm grateful to the possibly Slavic girl for describing something I have experienced—because if this is a pattern, if there is a way that alcoholics from all over the world behave, maybe it wasn't that Lucy didn't love me enough to quit. Maybe all of this was not really her choice (which is to say *not really her fault*).

Gavin says he's been in the program for almost twenty years; he started coming after his brother drank himself to death. He was demolished by the loss. At the first meeting Gavin attended, someone read something that gave him a flash of solace: "Just for today, I will adjust myself and not try to manipulate the situation." He had spent years trying to persuade his family that there was something wrong. But his brother was gone now, and that could not be changed, no matter what Gavin did or said. He opened his mind to the possibility that, really, it had never mattered. The situation, his brother's drinking, their parents' response, had all always been beyond his control.

I think about all the time I spent vigilant, preoccupied, trying to decipher my mother's relationship with Marcus, Lucy's relationship with alcohol. It had never occurred to me that both situations were whatever they were, whether I figured them out or not. And it had certainly never crossed my mind that my reaction—my suffering—was *mine*: something I had come up with, not something I needed to blame on anyone else.

My job is to interpret, and to communicate my interpretation persuasively to other people. The idea that in life, unlike in writing, the drive to analyze and influence might be something worth relinquishing was to me a revelation.

26

"I WAS SEVENTEEN WHEN I GOT CONSCRIPTED INTO THE army," Dr. John writes. "I did a year and a half, then got an early release to go to medical school (which is why I ended up a doctor and not a veterinarian, which is what I really wanted to be). I was slowly coming to realize that I was fighting on the wrong side, so early release sounded like an excellent idea. The army was largely very boring, in a 'not another fucking beautiful day in Africa' sort of way. When it wasn't boring you were getting shot at, so boring was generally preferable."

His favorite memory from that time was of swimming with some croupiers at the Victoria Falls Hotel when he was on leave. "I knew one girl well, she swam for the Rhodesia team, and the other girl was a vibrant redhead from England. The swimmer and I decided to head across to Cataract Island, which sits right in the middle of the falls . . . it's spectacular, because you can go and stand on the edge and peer straight over the precipice, with huge volumes of water rushing past on both sides. To reach the island, you have to swim strongly across a section called Devil's Cataract. Unfortunately, the English girl decided to follow us. We were over halfway across when this redhead went bobbing past, not making headway and obviously on her way straight over the edge of the falls. I swam after her and managed to drag her to the island, but we only just made it. It was *really* hair-raising: your eyes are at water level so you can't see what's going on but the water is going faster and faster and things are getting really noisy and turbulent and you can just feel this unbelievably massive power sucking at you. And all the time I am trying to decide 'when am I going to let this woman go and just swim for it myself?' But as you can imagine, that's a very difficult decision to make, and fortunately I didn't have to make it."

I think of Norman Rush's novel *Mating*, and his description of approaching Victoria Falls: "Well before you see water you find yourself walking through pure vapor. The roar penetrates you and you stop thinking without trying." His protagonist, a tough, lost American woman in her thirties, is "overcome with enormous sadness, from nowhere," when she first sees the falls, and finds herself weeping wildly. She is a fierce character, an erstwhile Ph.D. candidate in anthropology who has marooned herself in Africa, yearning to accomplish something substantive and "feeling sexually alert." At the falls, she has the urge to make herself "part of something magnificent and eternal, an eternal mechanism," by casting herself into the avalanche of water.

"I started to edge even closer, when the thought came to me If you had a companion you would stay where you are." This revelation destabilizes her. "Where was my companion? I had no companion, et cetera. I had no life companion, but why was that?"

My companion is gone. Where is Dr. John's companion? I think about how such a woman would dress and talk, what she would know and want.

"After that, things got comical," his email continues. "A spotter plane had seen all this going on and alerted the army, so the whole battalion, including my commanding officer, was standing on the banks of the Zambezi watching us make our way back. The English girl had lost her bikini bottom somewhere in the process (and as I mentioned she was a *very* vibrant redhead) so I felt obliged to lend her my swim trunks. Getting back entailed making our way over to the Zambian side and then walking up-river on the bank before swimming across. So there I was, a stark-naked white Rhodesian army boy escorting two girls in what was essentially enemy territory, being watched through a pair of binoculars by my commanding officer. It was on the eve of a leave period for me, which got canceled as punishment. That ended up being fortunate, because the following night a platoon of ours got ambushed and sustained heavy casualties, so having an extra medic they could fly in was useful. The rest of my war stories are really mundane and boring. Well, none of them involve red pubic hair, and I've always thought, 'What's the point of a story without that?' Haven't you?"

27

married can feel like slipping through the threads of the fabric of life. When there were two of you connected, you were big enough to stay suspended, but now you will fall through and plummet off the planet, alone. The risk is greatest when you are surrounded by intact couples and families. If you are among other single people and you feel yourself start to slip, there is always the possibility of grabbing on to another lone human.

A month before her due date, Emma gets married. The reception is at a little restaurant in Pasadena. We sit outside under strings of fairy lights, the pricking scent of jasmine penetrating the cool January night. Mercifully, the party is small—most of Emma's friends have come without their husbands and children, so it is as if time has turned back to the days when we were all single, when everyone was holding on to everyone else. I try hard not to drink too much or to cry.

Emma and I always acted as if I were the slightly more together one. I had an easier time getting boyfriends in college. I was more strategic and dogged about my career when we were in our twenties, and figuring out how to live as an adult seemed to require all of Emma's resources. We agreed on a narrative in which she was less adept at wringing what she wanted from the world.

But now here she is, eight months pregnant, bursting with life in a white lace dress. Her beauty holds your eyes: her sweet small teeth, her pale skin and dark curly hair, her ladylike hands resting on the balloon of her belly. During the ceremony at the temple, it seemed like a wedding not just between Emma and her husband, but between both of them and their baby. The rabbi referred to "the three of you" throughout the service.

I know that Emma feels bad about going into motherhood without me—I felt bad about going into lesbianism without her when I met my first girlfriend. We dislike being out of sync.

"Do we look alike?" she used to ask people in college.

"On a spectrum of heads," my father told her once, "you're not that far apart."

A girl at a bar in the East Village asked us, "Which one of you came up with the personality?" when we were jabbering at her one night soon after we moved to New York City. We loved that.

The last time I saw Emma before the wedding was in August, at the beach in Massachusetts, when we were each in our first trimester. Her mother, Margaret, has a carriage house in an eighteenth-century whaling village where the houses have little plaques by the doors stating the years they were built and the occupations of their first inhabitants: mariner; distiller; gentleman. We met there, as we have every summer since college. In the mornings we went walking past the fields of Queen Anne's lace. In the afternoons we drove to the beach, both swollen in our bathing suits. We discussed names, of course, but also holidays, birthdays, when she would come to New York and when I would visit her in Los Angeles, whether there was any chance the babies might dodge inheriting our hair, which is the same: curly like a sheep's.

We would be the godmothers of each other's children. We would raise them as cousins. We talked about what it would be like the following summer, sitting with them on a blanket and dangling their four feet in the sea.

My mother's house on Cape Cod is not far from there; she came to dinner that night and brought an oddly shaped piece of yellow fabric she'd woven on her loom for Emma to use as a burping cloth. Though Margaret has a South African accent and my mother retains a vaguely midwestern inflection, flecks of Yiddish float through both of their speech. They are the same size and shape (small, with fluffy silver heads of hair) and they both wear loose shirts and comfortable sandals. I watched them getting dinner ready together. It was easy to imagine our mothers in different clothes, in a previous generation, doing the same thing somewhere in Eastern Europe. None of us were very far from one another on a spectrum of heads.

At Emma's wedding, while we are eating the white cake together after my toast, she says, "Do you hate me for being pregnant?" And I tell her the truth. I feel that her child, in a lesser but still crucial way, will be mine, too.

LATE THAT NIGHT, Emma's parents and I sit on her couch looking at a map of South Africa on the computer. We zoom in on the street in Cape Town named after Margaret's aunt, Helen Suzman, the only female member of the South African parliament in her era, and, for thirteen years, the only member to oppose apartheid. (P. W. Botha called her a "vicious little cat.") Emma's father, Erroll, points out Muizenberg—"Jewsenberg," people used to call it, he says—the beach where he learned to surf, just outside the city. And not far from there, we find Sir Lowry's Pass, where Dr. John's horses are waiting for him at the foothills of the Hottentots Holland Mountains. "It's a very nice part of the world," Margaret says, in that crisp, familiar accent I was so surprised and relieved to hear in a Mongolian clinic a few months earlier. We look for images of the area on the Internet and see green cliffs rising out of the sea. I imagine what it would be like to ride a horse through those mountains, to grip an animal with your thighs and have no choice but to hold on and hope.

"The first time I really had a chance to ride was when I

was about six years old," John wrote me that morning. "We were on a coastal holiday in the Transkei at a secluded, slightly shabby resort. There's a strong indigenous horse culture in that area, mainly for cattle herding on the dirt roads. The resort had a string of retired and grumpy old ponies and some shoddy tack held together by string. I used to drag my brother Greg down there two, three times a day to saddle up and go riding; if I couldn't find him I would just go and hang out in the paddock on my own. One morning I wandered down there and as I wiggled through the fence they decided, as a herd, to come to me rather than the other way around. It was the first time I remember being truly happy after my mother died. One old mare leaned down very close and blew a gust of warm air from her huge nostrils straight into my face. I burst into tears. 'Look her in the eye and blow your soul into her nose,' a Xhosa groom told me later. I've done that with every horse I've met since."

He has three now: an old mare, a skinny white filly, and his favorite, a chestnut gelding. "The riding around Sir Lowry's Pass is great, there are miles of paths through the local vineyards and olive groves. If you were ever in the Cape for a while, I could teach you to ride. You would love it."

Though Margaret and Erroll grew up in overlapping social circles in the Jewish community in Johannesburg, though they'd both heard of each other and knew members of each other's families, they didn't start dating until they'd left home and crossed paths in the United States. We marvel at the unexpected ways people find each other.

28

·

WHEN I HEAR THAT SOMEONE HAS LUNG CANCER, *DID he smoke?* comes into my head midway between the syllables *can* and *cer.* Obviously I don't say it out loud, but I want to know, because I want to believe that if only my loved ones and I refrain from smoking, we will be ineligible for lung cancer (and, ideally, every other kind of cancer).

"Have they figured out what happened yet?" people keep asking me about my own medical defeat.

"Yes," I tell them. "I had bad luck."

That is not what they want to hear. They want to hear that I had a bad obstetrician. Or that I took something you are not supposed to take, or didn't take something that you are. They want to hear that I neglected to get an ultrasound. Or that I have some kind of rare blood disorder that can be fixed with the right medicine or surgery or iPhone app. They want to know what they have to eat to keep from being me.

And since I *have* done something that sounds bad,

people—even people who really love me—persist in saying things like "Next time, you're not getting on any planes." It doesn't matter if I tell them that every doctor I've consulted has said unequivocally that there's nothing wrong with flying when you're five months pregnant. They want to believe that everything happens for a reason.

Some people need to believe this to indemnify themselves—against miscarriage, or misfortune in general. Some people need to believe it so they can say, "You'll get pregnant again and everything will work out fine," because they want to comfort me.

But in a strange way, I *am* comforted by the truth. Death comes for us. You may get ten minutes on this earth or you may get eighty years but nobody gets out alive. Accepting this rule gives me a funny flicker of peace.

When I was in my early thirties I wrote a profile of Maureen Dowd. She was the sole female columnist at *The New York Times* then, and had been the second female White House correspondent in the paper's history. She had started her career as an editorial assistant in 1974, the year I was born, and now she was fifty-three, had won the Pulitzer Prize, looked amazing, and lived alone. I remember sitting in the insanely decorated living room of her brownstone in Georgetown—the walls were blood red, the bookshelves were crowded with feathered fans, old Nancy Sinatra record jackets, a collection of bubbling motion lamps, another of mermaids, a dozen vintage martini shakers, all kinds of toy tigers—and being intoxicated by her peculiarity, independence, and success.

I asked if she'd ever wanted children. She told me, "Everybody doesn't get everything."

It sounded depressing to me at the time, a statement of defeat. Now admitting it seems like the obvious and essential work of growing up. Everybody doesn't get everything: as natural and unavoidable as mortality.

29

A FANTASY: I FIND A STORY IN SOUTH AFRICA. SOMETHING
fantastic, that my mind wants to chew up. (I have been
reading about Julius Malema, the former head of the African National Congress Youth League, who inserted himself
into the Caster Semenya debacle. He has just been side-
lined by President Jacob Zuma, who was once his mentor,
but Malema still has avid support in the townships, and he
is about to go on trial for money laundering . . .) In my fantasy, I fly to Cape Town and Zerihun picks me up. We are
happy to see each other, excited by the reactivation of our
unlikely alliance. This time, I have plenty of contacts. We
are on the job.

But really, I'm on two. Dr. John and I plan to meet—
somewhere unfussy, with paper napkins. When we see each
other it's exciting but comfortable; words pour from our
mouths like they've flowed from our fingers onto the computer. We are connected, united. In my imagining, we
laugh easily, even though he is wry and old and dashing

and I am coarse and young(ish) and Jewish. Somehow, I feel lovely. I am not ungainly and leaking. I do not feel tears stirring in my sinuses. In his eyes (and therefore mine), there is still a coruscating light in me, I am not dead inside and I don't kill what's inside of me. The past is prelude and now we are leaving the restaurant and the fog is rolling out toward the Southern Ocean. When he kisses me, it feels natural, inevitable. It doesn't feel like a stranger has his mouth on mine; he doesn't taste old or male or alien.

I go to see his cottage, and it is just as he described it in his letters: "I keep my horse riding tack and saddles on wooden brackets mounted on one wall, and there is usually a surfboard leaning in a corner and a wetsuit hanging in the shower. When I added the wooden loft as a bedroom, I forgot to leave space for the staircase; it now has what is essentially a ladder going up the one side. Chickens roost in the chimney's ash trap and they emerge from their egg-laying speckled grey." It is a home, but a wild home, cheerful, peculiar—like Pippi Longstocking's Villa Villekulla, with a horse on the porch in an overgrown garden on the edge of town, where it "stood there ready and waiting for her."

And then what?

I move to South Africa? He teaches me to ride horses and I have his baby? I become a foreign correspondent! I start a whole new life, a life I never saw coming. Either that, or I am isolated and miserable, I've destroyed my career, and I spend my days gathering sooty chicken eggs.

A different fantasy: I fly to Cape Town. It is not as I remember it. It's just a place, not another state of being. I am panicky and agitated. I cry without warning, and once I start, I can't stop. It is not at all clear that my story will work out. Now I have lost my powers in that department, too.

Dr. John and I make a plan to meet. But in this fantasy, I arrive at the restaurant and find it intimidating and confusing: I don't know if I'm supposed to wait to be seated and I can't get anyone's attention. I'm afraid of being rude, wrong, American. When John arrives he is a stranger. I don't know him and I don't really like him, or worse, I can tell that he doesn't like me. Our conversation is stilted. I know (and he suspects) that I have come all this way for an encounter that isn't worth having, and a story that isn't worth telling, at least not by me. I have made myself ridiculous. My losing streak continues.

And yet. "I have never seen the great migrations. I've got a really old Land Rover that I've owned since 1986 (and it was old when I bought it). My dream has been to nurse it up through Africa one day—Cape to Cairo, or some version of that epic. Not that it is very reliable; I insist on doing all my own mechanical work, and that is so emphatically not a good idea. But breaking down can be very rewarding. Zen and the art of . . . that kind of thing."

Here is a third fantasy: I go. My story is real and I believe in my ability to tell it well. I meet him, but it's not a date. We become friends—we realize that we already are. I look up to him; I come to depend on his advice. He is like a big brother, like Neil Reardon or my editor John Homans (but with silver hair and blue eyes and stories about riding a horse to work in the Transkei to do Caesareans by candlelight). We keep writing to each other after I've finished my story and returned home.

We are strangely important to each other for the rest of our lives. In this fantasy, he comes to visit me in New York from time to time. A few years after our first meeting, I go with him from the Cape to Cairo in his Land Rover. My kid comes, too.

30

SOMETHING IS HAPPENING. SOMETHING VERY SMALL AND very new is sending up a shoot inside of me. It's a sprout of surrender that feels somehow indistinguishable from safety. It is not emanating from a plan. For the first time in my life, I have no plan.

I want it to grow. I want it to overcome me, like a bright vine swallowing a fading tree.

Also, *I want my son.*

I want to feel his mouth on my breast. I want to teach him the names of all the plants: *Alcea, Nepeta, Alchemilla, Cimicifuga.* I want to see him on his father's lap and in my mother's arms. I will never know another day when he isn't missing, missed. I want my son. But I can't have him.

For Lucy I feel more tenderness and intensity than I can fit inside my chest. She feels like kin—like blood. I don't want to be without her in this life. But our marriage is over. Slowly, we will become something else to each other.

I don't want to give up my home, the garden where I can

remember planting every flower, the circle of stones that marks Paolo's resting place, where he lies in an endless embrace with his sex bunny. But it isn't mine to keep.

I want to be fertile. I never want to expire.

But death comes for us.

What first? What else? What next?

As everything else has fallen apart, what has stayed intact is something I always had, the thing that made me a writer: curiosity. Hope.

31

THE NIGHT BEFORE I LEFT, AFRICA WAS GOLDEN AND
pulsating in my mind.

I emptied the wool socks and maternity jeans from my
suitcase, which I had shoved under the bed when I got back
from Mongolia. I packed hiking boots, a bathing suit, my
blue blazer for interviews, a stack of notepads, and the bat-
tered map of Cape Town I still had in a drawer with my
passport, an adaptor, and some stray rupees.

I called my mother the next morning from the airport,
anxious. She said, "Get on the plane. You will be fine."

Maybe. Maybe I would get a great story from this trip—
the best I'd ever written. Maybe not. Maybe I would fall in
love again, and I would still get to be a mother. Or maybe it
was too late, and I had already chosen, inadvertently and
incrementally, to be something else. In writing you can always change the ending or delete a chapter that isn't working. Life is uncooperative, impartial, incontestable.

I cried only once during the twenty-one-hour flight. I

was looking out the window at the moon and thinking of the last long trip I took across the sky, and of the person who went with me and didn't come back. For a while, it was as poisonous and wrenching as it had been since the day it happened, as intolerable: a crime against nature. Then the grief went back to sleep in my body. And it was again nature herself.

Nature. Mother Nature. She is free to do whatever she chooses.

ACKNOWLEDGMENTS

FOR THEIR GENEROSITY AND KINDNESS, I THANK JONA-than Adler, Mark Alhadeff, Anne Banchoff, Jesse Block-ton, Erica Malm Cooley, Jackson Cox, Simon Doonan, Benjamin Dreyer, Lauren Engel, Esther Fein, Daphne Fitzpatrick, Malcolm Gladwell, Erica Gonzalez, Alicia Gordon, Jenny Grant, Adam Green, Vanessa Grigoriadis, Cate Hartley, Julia Hine, Matt Hyams, London King, David Klagsbrun, Eric Konigsberg, Liz Lange, Shelly Levin, Robert Levy, Siobhan Liddell, Kate Medina, Debo-rah Needleman, Ed Pas, Beth Pearson, Anna Pitoniak, David Remnick, Meredith Rollins, Maer Roshan, Deb Schwartz, David Shapiro, Eric Simonoff, Annie Smith, Rene Steinke, Neil Tardio, Christine and Chuck Teggatz, Ahna Tessler, Jennie Thompson, Liz Thompson, Jacob Weisberg, David Zelman, Diana Zock, and Elisa Zonana. I would especially like to thank my friend Nick Trautwein.

ARIEL LEVY joined *The New Yorker* as a staff writer in 2008, and received the National Magazine Award for Essays and Criticism in 2014 for her piece "Thanksgiving in Mongolia." She is the author of the book *Female Chauvinist Pigs* and was a contributing editor at *New York* for twelve years.

ariellevy.net

@avlskies